GREAT BOUTIQUE

Wines

YOU CAN BUY ONLINE

MW00829837

CONTENTS

Welcome to *Great Boutique Wines You Can Buy Online*. Our goal here is to connect wine lovers like you with little known gems that are hard to find. With our combined 25 years in the wine business, we have made many friends who have wondered how to reach a wider audience. Now thanks to the internet, you have access to these gems. Whether organic, biodynamic, unusual varietals, or just plain great deals, the wines listed here are some of the best in the country. Most are from small, family-owned wineries with productions of around 5000 cases.

Our selection process was based on quality of the wine, first and foremost, and then internet availability. For our tastings, we employed the systematic, or deductive tasting process, the international standard in professional wine evaluation. This is the same procedure used by the Institute of Masters of Wine, the International Court of Master Sommeliers, the Culinary Institute of America—Rudd Center, Copia—The American Center for Wine, Food and the Arts, international wine competitions, wine evaluation labs, and countless others around the globe.

Since many of the included wineries are no more than "mom and pop" operations, they did have to have at a minimum a functioning website

with contact information to enable you to order their wines. Many have convenient order page/shopping cart features. You will also encounter several with a mailing list. With some wines counted in bottles produced, this is a small price to pay.

Rather than starting with chardonnay for white and cabernet sauvignon for red, we listed wines as you might see them on a restaurant wine list. Thus, you'll find lightest whites to fullest, then lightest reds to fullest. This is followed with a small selection of sweet and fortified wines. We only recommended one sparkling wine; production is very challenging at such a small scale. While there are many fine examples produced in the U.S., most of them come from wineries with 20,000 case production or higher.

Each wine listing follows the same format, with the winery information, winery profile, the recommended wine name and price, reason for selection, style, description, and special features illustrated with symbols.

We encourage you to try something new. Wine, like life, is an adventure. Take the plunge!

"We all need to remember that we pull a cork for sensual reasons and that sensual words best capture the experience."

— *Master Sommelier Joseph Spellman*

The online wine business is undergoing a revolution around the world. In Europe, direct shipment to the consumer is on the rise. Here in the U.S., there has never been a better time to discover, tour and taste the hundreds of great boutique/small production wineries of America, due in part to the recent United States Supreme Court ruling in *Granholm, Governor of Michigan, v. Heald*, and the fact that overnight shippers now ship wine in and out of approximately 30 states (see Appendix A on pages 232–233).

In the past, the only way for limited-production, or "boutique" wineries to promote their wine was to sell it to those fortunate few who found their way to the winemaker's door. Now, however, thanks to the gradual relaxation of wine shipping laws, hundreds of boutique wineries across America offer their wines online to millions of internet consumers.

What is direct shipment, and why is it so important?

The process by which wine is shipped from the producer to the consumer is called direct shipment. The relaxation of direct shipment laws is already having a significant impact on the wine industry, particularly boutique wineries, because it circumvents the three-tier system by which wine has traditionally been distributed to the consumer.

Traditionally, wine was imported or made at the winery and sold to a wholesaler, who in turn sold it to a retailer, who finally sold it to you, the consumer, with taxes added at every level. Direct shipment, however, enables the winery to sell directly to the consumer, thereby completely avoiding the three-tier process.

Not only is direct shipment great for consumers, but it's also very beneficial to the smaller, boutique wineries, whose production yields are too small to merit the attention of most distributors/wholesalers.

Where does the internet come in?

These days, it may be rare to order wine for dinner over the internet and have it shipped to one's home. Soon, however, this will be a very common practice. The internet is the perfect conduit for the process of direct wine sales, creating a direct and practically cost-free

link between winemakers and consumers. Within five years, ordering wine over the internet will be standard practice for millions of Americans.

What if my state doesn't allow direct shipment of alcoholic beverages?

States' laws are constantly changing. It is precisely for this reason that we have chosen to include in this book wineries from states whose laws still restrict their abilities to ship wine. Because these laws are still in a state of flux, it is very likely that over the next few years, more states will be added to the expanding list of states allowing direct shipment of wine, to the benefit of winemakers and consumers alike.

In the Appendix, you will find a simple chart with a summary of direct shipment laws in all 50 states. This chart should be used as a guide, but not as the final word on direct shipment. You will find a list of websites you can visit to see up-to-date laws and advice on how you can learn more about direct shipment in your home state.

You should also check with national shippers such as UPS and FedEx in your home state to see if direct shipment is allowed there. The final decision-maker in this process, of course, is the winery: hundreds ship direct right now to more than 30 states, and the number of boutique wineries that ship direct is ever increasing as this becomes an important winery profit center.

A toast to the beginning, a look to the future

Wine country is no longer limited to Napa Valley. Over the past few decades, wineries have sprung up in practically every state in the U.S. Now, thanks to the internet, you can enjoy virtual tours of wineries from Arizona to Alaska, from Napa Valley to New Jersey. From hundreds of these internet wine sites, you can order boutique wines and have them sent directly to your home without ever involving distributors and retailers.

This book is the recognition of a new beginning to internet wine buying. If you are reading this, congratulations. You are on the cutting edge of the next major trend in American wine.

Co-author Catherine Fallis, a Master Sommelier, shares these thoughts on wine:

Styles and Varietals

What is wine? It is one of the most enjoyable beverages on the planet. It is, even at its most sublime, though, the fermented juice of fresh, ripe grapes. Wine, like the human body, is approximately 90% water. The rest is made up of color, aroma, and flavor compounds, alcohol, acid, sugar, fruit tannins, wood tannins, and trace vitamins and minerals. Wine is commonly known as a healthful beverage when consumed regularly, in moderation, and with a meal, unless one is predisposed to alcoholism or other addictive traits.

Wine may be white, red, or rosé. Wine may be bone dry or decadently sweet. It may be still, sparkling, or fortified. Winemakers may ferment wines in inert vessels such as stainless-steel tanks or in oak barrels, most commonly from French or American forests. Further ageing of the wine may take place in barrels. American oak imparts sweet, tropical coconut, vanilla, and toast tones, while the French oak imparts more subtle vanilla and cedary tones.

In Europe, where unpredictable weather is a fact of life, many wines are made up of blends of more than one grape variety, with the resulting wines reflecting a traditional and regional, rather than varietally-driven, style. Winemakers hedge their bets, planting several varieties that will ripen over an eight to ten week period. Some ripen earlier, giving the winemaker a form of security if rains threaten to ruin the crop. For example, the red Bordeaux wines of France may be blended from cabernet sauvignon, cabernet franc, merlot, malbec, and petite verdot, thus giving us the name "Bordeaux Blend."

France's Rhone Valley is another great example of blends. Syrah is dominant in the north, with grenache, mourvedre, and many others used in the south. In this country, we have a strong following for both these red and the many white Rhone varietals, thus the "Rhone Blend" category.

Forward thinking Italian wine producers gave us the "Super-Tuscan Blend," going outside of their traditional grape requirements to bring us what they thought would be better wines. In the U.S., we call these "Cal-Ital" blends.

For the most part, though, you'll find American wines listed by their grape varietal. We don't say, "I'll have a Napa Valley," but instead, "I'll have a chardonnay." This is the same in warmer areas of the world as well, including in South America, Australia, and New Zealand.

The vine family, *Ampelidaceae*, includes the genus, *Vitis*, and its species: *amurensis, labrusca, riparia, rupestris* (St. George), *berlandieri, aestivalis, cinerea, rotundifolia, and vinifera. Vitis vinifera*, native to Europe and Central Asia, is responsible for 99.99% of the world's quality wine production.

Other species of the vine family are relevant as rootstock, progenitors of hybrids, or as alternative sources of wine. Producers of premium wine around the world look to *Vitis vinifera* grape varietals, including riesling, chenin blanc, sauvignon blanc, semillon, chardonnay, cabernet sauvignon, merlot, pinot noir, and syrah.

In areas with challenging climate conditions, such as much of the Eastern United States, winemakers rely on crosses and hybrids bred to withstand extremes of climate and disease. A cross is a vine variety bred from more than one variety of the same species. A hybrid is a new vine variety bred from members of more than one species.

Producers in New York State, for example, rely on *Vitis labrusca* grapes such as Concord, *labrusca*-parented (and thus American) hybrids such as Catawba, or pure French hybrids such as Vidal Blanc (Ugni Blanc x Seibel 4986) for their hardiness in winter.

> "A meal without wine is like a day without sunshine."
> — *Jean Anthelme Brillat-Savarin*

On Tasting

Tasting professionally is very different than tasting for fun. Professional tasting is just that. The wine is not swallowed in most cases, as the alcohol build up would tend to impair the evaluator. The best environment for the sterile, scientific evaluation process is a neutral one. Good lighting is critical. Plain white placemats or tablecloths provide the ideal background. Consistent glassware is best, and the international standard tasting glass is what I recommend (the INAO), though many prefer the more impressive, but less effective Riedel glassware. Perfumes, aftershaves, fragranced body lotions, and even some hair products provide enough distraction for the average nose to impair its ability to read what is in the glass. So do cooking or food smells. Glasses, by the way, should be completely odor free to begin with. The only way to guarantee this is to wash them with hot water only. No soap. No bleach. Just water. The best time to evaluate wines is first thing in the morning, before the senses are barraged. Hunger brings a heightened sensitivity and increases sensory perception.

Here is the method I work with most often, which is based on the deductive tasting process. For the first go-around, don't worry about all of the details. Practice first with the basic steps. Go at your own pace.

Use your senses. Note your sheer, visceral, bodily reactions. Don't think. Just react. You can do it! Use the following professional deductive tasting process as a jumping-off point, giving your tasting some structure. Don't worry too much about the details in the beginning. Over time, you'll become more and more comfortable with this system.

Step One—See

Open your eyes and look at the wine in your glass.

Look down into the glass at the disc or top. Think of this as a CD-Rom. Is it bright and shiny or perhaps a little cloudy? Swirl the glass; note the viscosity (thickness). Tilt the glass against a white surface and look at and through the color. Hold two fingers under the bowl of the glass. How clearly can you see them through the color? Is the

color consistent from the center of the glass to the edge (from the center ring of the CD out to the rim) or is there some variation?

Appearance

Brightness

Viscosity

Color/hue

Depth of color

Color variation from center to rim

Be cool. Swirl your glass without spilling any.

Step Two—Smell
Take a whiff, but don't inhale.

Aroma

First impressions

Is it clean?

Does is smell sweet or dry?

Fruit

Alcohol (high alcohol feels like a little hammer hitting your forehead between the eyebrows)

Wood (vanilla, caramel, woodfire, smoke, char, toast smells)

Maturity (obvious fruity characters fade with age)

Grape variety/varieties

Tip: To get more serious, check out The Wine Aroma Wheel *from A. C. Noble. For more information email acnoble@ucdavis.edu or call (530) 752-0387 to order.*

Step Three—Taste and Touch

Take a sip.

Chew on it.

Gargle it.

Spit it out.

Warning: Practice this at home only. Gargling wine in public may lead to a quick exit by your dinner companion.

Palate

First impressions – tactile impressions (what does it feel like?)

Confirm nose (does it smell like you expected it to?)

Alcohol (high alcohol gives richness and a sweet impression)

Acidity (is it tingly, tart, racy, or mellow?)

Dryness/sweetness

Wood (astringency, drying character?)

Tannin (from wood, from fruit?)

Texture (austere, tart, chewy, smooth, supple?)

Intensity (this is not an indication of quality)

Ripeness (this is a hint as to origin and quality)

Flavor (what does it taste like?)

Balance (if nothing stands out, and the components are well-integrated, it is balanced and of good quality.)

Persistence/length, "finish" (the longer the aftertaste, the better the quality)

Quality level (Is it balanced and reflective of its origin? Is it of commercial, everyday, premium, or super-premium quality?)

Just imagine if you worked at an ice cream parlor all summer. Each day at work you'd taste several flavors. By the end of summer, you could blind taste and recognize most of the aromas and flavors and let out a steady stream of beautiful descriptors simply because you spent the last few months getting to know them. You'd have become an ice cream expert! The same applies to wine. Familiarity breeds confidence.

Wine Styles, Varietals, and Professional Tasting excerpted with the permission of Catherine Fallis, from the *grape goddess guides to good living* series. ©Planet Grape. World Rights Reserved.

High Rollers Not Fit for the Table

On a first date in Napa Valley this summer, my dinner companion arrived with a bottle of Napa syrah provided by his host. I gently explained the two reasons I didn't think it was appropriate to open it. First of all, it was on the wine list. Second of all, I had no intention of obliterating my palate. I was excited about the food, and was determined to enjoy a balanced wine that would flatter it, not some super-ripe, concentrated, tannic monster.

Pity the man who thinks he can win me over with modern wine. Am I old-fashioned? You bet. Am I unfashionable in my wine tastes? Yes, sir. Will I give up lacy riesling and tart, mouth-puckering pinot noir to drink killer cab and monster zin? I think not.

Wine has intrinsic tartness. This is one of the reasons it has graced dinner tables for so many centuries; tartness serves to stimulate the gastric juices as well as to cleanse the palate between bites. However, many of today's most highly rated wines are crafted to please the palate without the benefit of food. While enjoyable on their own as cocktails, these 100-point, blockbuster-style wines are unbalanced and generally unsuitable for the table. They are donut wines—flashy, fruity, and creamy on the outside, with nothing inside.

A handful of wineries are bucking the trend of making boozy cocktail wines, instead making wines that are subtle, understated, compatible with food, and capable of aging.

Chateau Montelena owners Jim and Bo Barrett say, "We're going to make a wine that is compatible with food and will improve with age, not a boozy chardonnay."

Robert Mondavi, on his 90th birthday, said, "Densely fruity California wines that are popular with wine critics are like high-end call girls with a lot of glitter."

New York Times writer Frank Prial agrees. He says, "California chardonnays are vinous SUVs. They're over-oaked and over-flawed."

With today's wine, the louder, richer, and deeper in color, the better. With spicy dishes, it seems like the hotter a wine is, the more highly regarded it is. Certainly as our senses are barraged, we lose the ability to enjoy subtlety and nuance of flavor, of music, of perfume, of art.

The biggest issue is whether or not Americans want wine to go with food or wine as a cocktail. As wine director at Aqua, a high-end seafood restaurant in San Francisco, I came into contact with Americans from all walks of life. I loved the guys who would puff out their chests and ask me questions like, "Should we start with the Opus One or the Joseph Phelps Insignia?" I'd choose one at random. What did it matter which beefy, tannic, complex red wine they had with their oysters, and ceviche? In my days of innocence, I would stop by the table with complimentary tastes of tchacoli, vinho verde, albarino, or a white friulian wine to have with the cold seafood platter. After a while I just gave up. People want what they want. My job was to make sure they got it.

Tim Meinken, co-owner of Sapphire Hill Vineyards & Winery in the Russian River Valley says, "One of the reasons we are getting higher alcohols is young vines with tight spacing."

Rick Hutchinson, owner and winemaker at Amphora Winery in Dry Creek Valley, adds, "Young vines want to take off and grow. Pruning, crop level, tight spacing for maximum efficiency of the soil, clones— they are all choices. Pinot noir at 16% alcohol is not a dinner wine."

Every winemaker's goal is to extract color, aroma, flavor, fruit tannins, and sugar from healthy, fully mature, ripe grapes, and then to finish the wine as he or she sees fit and as the style of wine dictates. The skilled winemaker seeks a seamless wine where all components are in balance, with no one component rising above the others. Ultimately, the passionate, artistic winemaker will stand in the fringes as his or her personal style doesn't conform.

A winemaker can manipulate for desired balance and extraction at all points, including enhancing or reducing alcohol, acid, or sugar; by selection of yeasts, by using temperature or SO_2 to enhance extraction, by employing malolactic fermentation, by choice of fermentation, and aging vessels. It can also be done by using techniques such as settling, racking, exposing to oxygen, exposing to SO_2, fining, cold stabilization, and filtering. Finally, a winemaker may blend finished wines from different lots, barrels or grape varieties to further achieve desired balance, and extraction.

Henri Jayer, producer of rare and highly sought-after ECHEZEAUX, VOSNE-ROMANEE CROS PARANTOUX, and VOSNE-ROMANEE LES BEAUMONTS, taught a generation of COTE DE NUITS producers to gain aroma and bouquet more gently and beneficially with an extended pre-fermentative cold soak.

His noninterventionist approach—unthinkable to many technologically minded winemakers—includes destemming, doing an extended pre-fermentative maceration in which the grapes are cooled to 15°C for five to seven days, encouraging the release of fine aromas and color, then crushing and macerating in the skins for up to 30 days.

The resulting wines are profound, mysterious, elusive, and immensely pleasurable to both the senses and the intellect, and are a delight with food.

Skilled, passionate winemakers strive to achieve both balance, and extraction in their wines. A New World winemaker has all the incentives to push for opaque color, dense tannin extraction and chart-topping alcohol, and may use all the tools in his or her arsenal to achieve this. In contrast a classic, traditional Old World producer may rely more on natural benefits such as terroir, and take a noninterventionist role to produce more long-lived, understated wines. Either way, they both rely on using the healthiest grapes their vineyards can produce and the many techniques at their disposal in the winery.

Ultimately, consumers will decide if the wines of massively high extraction are balanced enough for them to consume, let alone to

cellar. In the meantime, I'll be inviting more food-friendly wines to join me at the dinner table.

High Rollers Not Fit for the Table excerpted from *Wines & Vines magazine*, December, 2004, by Catherine Fallis. ©2004 Hiaring Company. ©2005 Gale Group.

Legend

Family Owned: Owned and operated by a single family.

Organic: An environmentally-friendly way of farming grapes and producing wines. For the USA, "Organic" wines have no added sulfites. "Organically-grown" wines allow up to 100 parts per million (ppm) of sulfur dioxide for use as an antioxidant. Both uses are under the control of the USDA National Organic Standards as well as state agencies (CCOF in California for example). Where used in this book, this symbol refers to "Organically grown" wines.

Biodynamic: Biodynamic principles are the most extreme form of alternative viticulture and winemaking, and emphasize not only the health and balance of the soil and plant, but of those working with it as well. Demeter is the most well known and highly regarded of the international certifying organizations. Where used in this book, the symbol refers to Demeter-certified wines.

Note: Where used in this book, "sustainable farming" refers to the practice of avoiding any form of environmental degradation. Chemical usage is not regulated, nor is the phrase "sustainable farming," with the notable exception of the groundbreaking Lodi Sustainable Viticulture Program.

Anglim Winery

740 Pine Street
Paso Robles, CA 93446
(805) 227-6813
www.anglimwinery.com

Owned and operated by Steve and Steffanie Anglim, Anglim Winery sources its grapes from Fralich Vineyard and French Camp Vineyard in Paso Robles and from the Bien Nicido Vineyard in Santa Maria. They produce only 2000 to 3000 cases per year.

Anglim Roussanne 2004, Paso Robles, $22

Good varietal expression. 100 cases produced.

Medium-bodied, dry.

Aromas of apricot, lemon zest, and apple. Tangy and fruity, with green apple, French oak, and mineral notes leading into a crisp finish. Great with fried calamari or steamed mussels.

Bray Vineyards

10590 Shenandoah Road
Post Office Box 87
Plymouth, CA 95669
(209) 245-6023
www.brayvineyards.com

Bray Vineyards was established in 1996. Less than half of the 50 acres are planted to vineyards from which barbera, cabernet sauvignon, sangiovese, tempranillo, zinfandel, black muscat, and alicante bouschet are produced.

Bray Vineyards Verdelho 2005, Lodi, $14

One of only a handful of U.S. versions. 264 cases produced.

Medium-bodied, dry.

Ginger ale, cream soda, lychee, lime zest, and musk notes. Bold and lemony with brisk acidity. Tart finish. Enjoy with oysters, fried calamari, or with chips and dip.

Calcareous Vineyard

3430 Peachy Canyon Road
Paso Robles, CA 93446
(805) 239-0289
www.calcareous.com

After selling his wine and beer distributing business in Sioux City, Iowa, Lloyd Messer moved out to Paso Robles and established the 442-acre Calcareous Vineyard in 2000. His daughter, Dana Brown, also sold her Iowa wine distributing business and joined him with her little sister Erika, making this a rare father-daughter operated winery. Justin Kahler is the winemaker.

Calcareous Roussanne 2004, Paso Robles, $24

Unique style.

Medium-bodied, dry.

Fruity aromas of orange, lemon, and honey, with a touch of pineapple. Smooth and creamy, with citrus, and oak notes. Excellent with pecan-crusted fried chicken or with soft, nutty cheeses.

Cass Vineyards and Winery

7350 Linne Road
Paso Robles, CA 93446
(805) 239-1730
www.casswines.com

Opened by Steve Cass in 2005, Cass Vineyards produces 100% estate-grown wines. The winery specializes in Rhone varietals and conducts cooking classes focusing on fare from around the world.

Cass Vineyards Roussanne Estate Grown 2005, Paso Robles, $24

An excellent 100% roussanne.

Light-bodied, off-dry.

Aromas of apple, pineapple, orange blossom, and oak. Smooth mouth-feel, with notes of rose petals, buttered toast and asparagus, and a lemony tingle at the finish. Enjoy it with mahi-mahi and grilled pineapple.

Chateau Lasgoity

11219 Road 26
Madera, CA 93637
(559) 674-8291
www.chateaulasgoity.com

Brother and sister team, John and Michele Lasgoity own and operate this winery located on the land purchased by their great-grandparents in 1903. Blanc du Val (White of the Valley) was their first wine, released in 2000, followed by merlot, syrah, and a rosé of zinfandel. The bulk of the fruit comes from the Lasgoity Family Ranches.

Chateau Lasgoity Blanc du Val 2004, Madera, $9

A refreshing change of pace.

Light-bodied, dry.

This blend of French colombard, malvasia bianco, and chardonnay has rose, orange peel, pear, apple and musky notes with a crisp palate, and a sweet-sour finish. Delicious with shrimp scampi, fresh cracked crab, or grilled peaches on lightly dressed greens with almond and mandarin orange slivers.

Chrisman Mill Vineyards & Winery

2385 Chrisman Mill Road
Nicholasville, KY 40356
(859) 881-5007
www.chrismanmill.com

In 1997, winemaker Chris Nelson and his wife Denise established Chrisman Mill. Since their first crush in 1999, their annual production has grown to about 3500 cases of primarily French American hybrids and non-*vinifera* grapes.

Chrisman Mill White Blend Ensemble (vidal blanc/seyval blanc) 2002, Kentucky, $14

Unusual blend of hybrids vidal blanc and seyval blanc.

Light-bodied, off-dry.

Aromas of pineapple, kiwi, and mango. Layers of tropical fruit and toasted oak, with a rich, buttery finish. Delicious with cracked crab and drawn butter.

Ciccone Vineyard & Winery

10343 East Hilltop Road
Suttons Bay, MI 49682
(231) 271-5553
www.cicconevineyards.com

Owned and operated by Silvio Tony Ciccone—also known as the father of Madonna—and his wife Joan, Ciccone Vineyards is one of a growing number of wineries in Michigan's relatively temperate Leelanau Peninsula. They produce about 2200 cases per year of over a dozen varietals, all harvested and crafted by hand.

Ciccone Pinot Grigio Blend Nectar (61% pinot grigio, 39% chardonnay) 2004, Leelanau Peninsula, Michigan, $15

Good value.

Medium-bodied, dry.

Aromas of pear, citrus, and spice. Creamy and buttery on the palate. Notes of stone-pit fruits, apple, citrus, and toasty oak, with a crisp finish. Great with seared tuna fillets or chicken stir-fry.

Clos Saron

Post Office Box 1004
Oregon House, CA 95962-1004
(530) 692-1080
www.clossaron.com

Gideon Beinstock and his wife Saron Rice specialize in pinot noir and non-traditional red and white blends in a high-altitude location in the Sierra Foothills. Sustainable farming is practiced.

Clos de Saron Carte Blanche 2005, California, $20

Good value. 894 bottles produced.

Medium-bodied, dry.

This blend of 55% viognier, 28% chardonnay, and 17% sauvignon blanc has peach, apricot, lemon, pink grapefruit, almond, and honey notes. Rich and creamy but very brisk and refreshing at the same time. A new twist in white wine. Enjoy with a salad of crab, spring peas, and vine ripened tomatoes with Dijon/shallot vinaigrette.

Fanucchi Vineyards

Post Office Box 290
Fulton, CA 95439
(707) 526-3219
www.fanucchivineyards.com

Peter Fanucchi began his career in wine in 1972, working alongside his father in the vineyard and winery crafting traditional wines mainly from century-old zinfandel vines. In 1992, he started his own label using fruit from the Fanucchi Wood Road Vineyard (sustainable farming is practiced). Today his old-vine zinfandel as well as trousseau gris, an aromatic white, are highly sought after by those in the know.

Fanucchi Vineyards Trousseau Gris The Fanucchi Wood Road Vineyard 2004, Russian River Valley, $14

A unique grape originally from Alsace and this is one of the only examples in the U.S.

Light-bodied, dry.

Hay, melon, peach, apple, banana, lemon, pine, and muscat-like orange blossom notes. Bright lemony and creamy palate with vibrant acidity. Enjoy with ceviche or fish tacos.

Giessinger Winery

365 Santa Clara Street
Fillmore, CA 93015
(805) 524-5000
www.giessingerwinery.com

Giessinger Winery was born in a converted welder's shop near Fillmore's old train depot in 1997. Owner and winemaker Eduoard Giessinger teaches wine tasting classes at U.C. Santa Barbara.

Giessinger Pinot Blanc 2002, Monterey County, $23

A classic expression of the varietal. Good value.

Medium-bodied, dry.

Crisp and dry, with notes of orange, citrus, pear, kiwi, and oak. Long, zesty finish. Try it with Asian-spiced chicken in wonton cups with apricot sauce.

Grey Bear Vineyards

25992 Highway T
Stover, MO 65078
(573) 377-4313
www.greybearvineyards.com

After ten years as the owner of Rocky Hill Winery in Montrose, Colorado, David Fansler founded Grey Bear Vineyards in 2003 and reopened in the spring of 2005. David's colorful past is echoed in the names of his wines—Bushwhacker, Chicks & Tiggers, and Indian Maiden, to name a few. Today he produces about 1300 cases of *vinifera* and French American hybrids a year.

Grey Bear Vignoles 2005, Missouri, $12

Often compared to chardonnay, but with its own unique style.

Medium-bodied, off-dry.

Toasty and fruity aromas. Notes of apple, peach, clover honey, and straw, with a long, buttery finish. Try it with Southern fare such as fried pork chops and hot buttered cornbread.

Haak Wine

6310 Avenue T
Santa Fe, TX 77510
(409) 925-1401
www.haakwine.com

Owner and winemaker Raymond Haak, who has a background in electrical engineering, began growing grapes in 1969. It was not until 1994, however, that he and his wife Gladys decided to turn their hobby into a commercial operation. They now produce about 5000 cases a year in their Mediterranean-style winery, which offers "a taste of the old world in Galveston County."

Haak White Table Wine Blanc du Bois 2005, Texas Gulf Coast Region, Texas, $13

An approachable Southern hybrid developed at the University of Florida for growing in warm climates.

Light-bodied, off-dry.

Tart and refreshing, with green apple, apricot, toast and melon notes, and a fresh finish. Take it on a picnic and serve with egg salad or club sandwiches.

August Hill Winery

106 Mill Street
Utica, IL 61373
(815) 667-5211
www.augusthillwinery.com

Owned by longtime friends Sean Ginocchio and Mark Wenzel along with Mark's wife Teri, August Hill Winery was born in 2000 when Mark inherited the family farmland. Mark shares winemaking duties with Sean's brother Christian.

August Hill Chardonel 2004, Illinois, $20

Immediately appealing.

Medium-bodied, off-dry.

Aromas of apricot, honey, and orange blossom. Stone-pit fruit and light citrus notes, with a round mouth-feel, and a buttery finish. Try it with cold pasta salad and sliced ham.

Winery of the Little Hills

501 South Main Street
St. Charles, MO 63301
(636) 946-9339
www.little-hills.com

David and Tammy Campbell purchased the Little Hills property in 1986, until which time it had served as a tavern. The winery currently produces about 1500 cases per year of French hybrids and non-*vinifera* wines.

Little Hills Chardonel 2003, Missouri, $18

Great expression of this hybrid of the famed chardonnay grape and seyval blanc.

Medium-bodied, dry.

Fresh citrus aromas with underlying tones of apple and oak. Citrusy and buttery on the palate, with green apple, pear, and lemon zest notes. Clean finish. Excellent with homemade chicken pot pie.

Peay Vineyards

1117B South Cloverdale Boulevard, #172
Cloverdale, CA 95425
(415) 531-2756
www.peayvineyards.com

Andy Peay, his brother Nick, and Nick's wife Vanessa Wong fell in love with this 48-acre vineyard in the far reaches of northwestern Sonoma after a long search for the perfect site. Vanessa, Nick's wife, earned her stripes as winemaker at Peter Michael, while Nick worked at Newton. She is winemaker, he is in charge of the vineyards, and Andy, MBA in hand, oversees sales and marketing. They specialize in syrah, pinot noir (William Selyem is a customer), viognier, and have 0.4 acres of roussanne and 0.2 acres of marsanne. Sustainable farming practices are in place.

**Peay Vineyards Roussanne/Marsanne Estate
2004, Sonoma Coast, $34**

Handcrafted to reflect origin and essence of the varietals.
90 cases produced.

Medium-bodied, dry.

Peachy, nutty, floral, herb tea, and mineral notes. Silky and fragrant
with vibrant acidity. Delicious with scallops in cream sauce, mushroom
risotto, and Munster or Gouda cheeses.

Marilyn Remark-Burnstein Remark Winery

645 River Road
Salinas, CA 93908
(831) 455-9310
www.remarkwines.com

Marilyn Remark and Joel Burnstein love Rhone grape varietals for
their compatibility with the Mediterranean diet. He was a former
stock trader. Today they produce roussanne, marsanne, rosé,
grenache, petite sirah, and syrah.

**Marilyn Remark Marsanne Loma Pacific Vineyard
2004, Monterey County, $30**

Benchmark wine. One of the best in the country.

Medium-bodied, dry.

White peach, lemon, banana, kiwi, star fruit, nilla wafer, and nutty
notes. Creamy and silky with excellent balance. Delicious with goat
cheese tarts topped with grilled onions and fig.

Silver Springs Winery LLC

4408 State Route 414
Burdett, NY 14818
(607) 351-8019
www.silverspringswinery.com

Proprietors Sari and John Zuccarino whose family originates in Udine, Italy, settled on Seneca Lake and released their first wines in 2002. They specialize in merlot, cabernet franc, catawba, and Delaware blends available in off-dry and sweet styles.

Silver Springs Winery Cayuga White 2004, Seneca Lake, New York, $10

Great for white zin fans and picnics.

Medium-bodied, off dry.

Pleasantly fruity with apple, pear, pineapple, sea spray, and pine needle notes. Creamy palate with a pithy, lychee finish. Enjoy with a Fontina or Gruyère and black forest ham panini, or with fresh apricots and mixed nuts.

Summerwood Winery

2175 Arbor Road
Paso Robles, CA 93446
(805) 227-1365
www.summerwoodwine.com

After earning a degree in enology from Fresno State University, Summerwood winemaker Scott Hawley studied with winemakers from around the world to develop his craft. He creates rich, intense wines that reflect the unique Paso Robles terroir.

Summerwood Diosa Blanc 2004 (60% roussane, 40% viognier), Paso Robles, $42

A beautifully aromatic and unique blend from the Templeton Gap.

Medium-bodied, dry.

Bursting with aromas of tropical fruit and sweet French oak. Mouthwatering notes of melon, pineapple, and lychee, with a fresh finish. Easily stands alone as an aperitif or with grilled halibut steaks served "al fresco."

Vahling Vineyards

Rural Route 1, Box 51
Stewardson, IL 62463
(217) 682-5409
https://medusa.ntsecure.net/vahlingvineyards/index_orig.htm

Dennis and Brenda Vahling opened Vahling Vineyards in 2002 on 2.5 acres in South Central Illinois. With the help of their family, they make about 2000 cases per year of hybrid, non-*vinifera*, and fruit wines, including traminette, seyval blanc, and mead.

Vahling Traminette 2004, Illinois, $12

Good example of this cold-tolerant hybrid. Some say it is similar to gewürztraminer.

Light-bodied, off dry.

Fresh and fruity, with aromas of apricot, lemon, and minerals. Flavors of sweet apricots, almonds, and wet stones. Excellent with crab cakes and tartar sauce.

Ventosa Vineyards

3440 Route 96A
Geneva, NY 14456
(315) 719-0000
www.ventosavineyards.com

Owners Lenny and Meg Cecere opened their Geneva winery in October 2005 with the help of consultant Rob Thomas, owner of Shalestone Vineyards in Lodi, Seneca County. They focus on Bordeaux varietals as well as riesling, vidal, and chardonnay.

Ventosa Vidal-Riesling 2005, Finger Lakes, New York, $15

Unique blend.

Light-bodied, dry.

This 60% vidal and 40% riesling wine has peach, caramel, and tangy Granny Smith apple notes. Tart, clean, and brisk. Delicious with oysters.

Westbrook Wine Farm

49610 House Ranch Road
O'Neal's, CA 93645
(559) 868-3499
www.westbrookwinefarm.com

Located near the southern entrance of Yosemite National Park in Madera County, this vineyard and "winery" center around a humble wooden shack belonging to Ray and Tammy Krause. They practice sustainable farming and minimalist winemaking.

Westbrook Wine Farm Viognier/Valdiguie 2005, Madera County, $16

Completely unique.

Medium-bodied, dry.

This blend of half viognier and half valdiguie is chardonnay-like in texture with vibrant peach, lemon, guava, Meyer lemon, banana pudding, butter, and vanilla notes. Delicious with braised pork with apples or as a cocktail.

J. Wilkes

342 Oliver Road
Santa Barbara, CA 93109
(805) 899-2845
www.jwilkes.com

Jeff Wilkes spent 18 years in marketing at Bien Nacido Vineyards before he and his wife Kimberly decided to open J. Wilkes in 2001. During that time, he learned the potential of Bien Nacido Vineyards for making high quality pinot noir, and for the first few years he and Kimberly focused on crafting only BNV pinot noir grapes. They have since begun to source grapes from a few other vineyards, and in 2004 they added pinot blanc.

J. Wilkes Pinot Blanc Bien Nacido Vineyards 2004, Santa Maria Valley—Santa Barbara, $18

An exceptionally lively pinot blanc, a natural mutation of the pinot noir grape.

Light-bodied, dry.

Bursting with floral and citrus aromas. Creamy and light on the palate, with crisp apple, pear, and lemon notes. Delicious with grilled chicken flavored with tarragon and lemon.

Brennan Vineyards

802 South Austin Street
Post Office Box 399
Comanche, TX 76442
(325) 356-9100
www.brennanvineyards.com

Owned by the Brennan family, Brennan Vineyards is located in the
McCrary House in Comanche, Texas a limestone house built in 1879.
They purchased the property in 1997 and decided shortly thereafter to
grow grapes on 33 adjacent acres. Together with the Wilkerson family,
they are celebrating their first release this year.

Brennan Muscat Reddy Vineyards 2005, Texas Hill Country, Texas, $11

Good value.

Light-bodied, off-dry.

Floral and tropical fruit aromas. Fresh and fruity, with pineapple,
melon, and green pea notes. Delicious with Chinese takeout or creamy
desserts such as crème brûlée.

La Sirena Wine

Post Office Box 441
Calistoga, CA 94515
(707) 942-1105
www.lasirenawine.com

Winemaker and owner Heidi Peterson Barrett of Screaming Eagle fame
says "La Sirena means "the mermaid" in Spanish and Italian. I chose
it because I was looking for something fun and magical (like wine)
and because I love to scuba dive as well as make wine."

La Sirena Moscato Azul 2005, Napa Valley, $30

Most muscat is made into sweet, dessert wine. This is a completely
unique expression of the varietal. Only 265 cases produced.

Full-bodied, dry.

Perfumed, floral and tropical with white peach, lychee, and pineapple
notes. Delicious with spicy dishes with Asian, Indian, or Thai influences.

Casa de Caballos Vineyards

2225 Raymond Avenue
Templeton, CA 93465
(805) 434-1687
www.casadecaballos.com

Tom and Sheila Morgan planted their first grapes on what was then
known as Morgan Farms in 1981. Within a few years, their planting
area had grown to about six acres, and they decided to bond and
rename the winery. Today they raise Arabian horses alongside their grapes.

Casa de Caballos Fantasy Riesling Blend (85% white riesling, 15% muscat canelli) 2005, $15

A touch of muscat gives this riesling added character and depth.
58 cases produced.

Light-bodied, off-dry.

Crisp and fruity, with lightly sweet notes of peach, pear, lime, and
sweet oak. Clean, refreshing finish. Excellent with Chinese honey-
battered prawns and pecans, or try it with a fresh fruit salad.

Cathedral Ridge Winery

4200 Post Canyon Drive
Hood River, OR 97031
(541) 386-2882
www.cathedralridgewinery.com

Owned by Robb Bell, Cathedral Ridge Winery (formerly Flerchinger
Vineyards) is located in an area of Oregon known for beautiful views
and windsurfing as well as for premium wine. The winemaker is
Mike Sebastiani.

Cathedral Ridge Riesling 2005, Columbia Gorge, Oregon, $12

A great white wine for aging.

Medium-bodied, dry.

Light floral and stone-pit fruit aromas. Apricot, rose petal, spice, and
mineral notes, with firm acids and a long, buttery finish. Try it with
light cheeses and cold cuts or with honey-baked ham.

Chateau Lafayette Reneau

Route 414
Hector, NY 14841
(607) 546-2062
www.clrwine.com

Dick and Betty Reno own and operate this lakeshore winery and inn (it is located in Hector on the east shore of Seneca Lake). Winemaker Tim Miller and vineyard manager oversee production of a full line of red and white premium wines.

Chateau Lafayette Reneau Dry Riesling 2005, Finger Lakes, New York, $14

Dry riesling fans buy this by the case. Excellent value.

Medium-bodied, dry.

Chalk, slate, pear, green delicious apple, lemon peel, and mandarin orange notes. Dry, racy, and pithy with a long, tart pink grapefruit/chalky finish. Delicious with oysters, Asian-styled grilled salmon, or smoked pork chop (or a grilled hot dog) with sauerkraut.

Chateau Lafayette Reneau Johannisberg Riesling 2005, Finger Lakes, New York, $14

Bracing backbone of acidity.

Medium-bodied, off dry.

Pineapple husk, guava, Meyer lemon, and honey notes. The slight bit of residual sugar softens and rounds out the palate but underneath is still a steely, racy, acidic wine. Delicious with hoisin barbecued chicken and grilled vegetables with chutney.

Esterlina Vineyards

1200 Holmes Ranch Road
Post Office Box 2
Philo, CA 95466
(707) 895-2920
www.esterlinavineyards.com

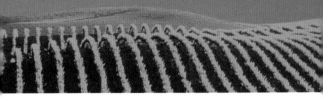

For several generations the Sterling family has been producing small lots of handcrafted wines from some of California's best vineyards. Today production centers around grapes grown in the family's estate vineyards which include the entire Cole Ranch American Viticultural Area (AVA).

Esterlina Off Dry Riesling 2005, Cole Ranch— Mendocino, $18

From America's only family-owned appellation.

Medium-bodied, dry.

Citrus, green apple, lime, honey, and mineral notes. Bracing acidity balanced by soft fruity sweetness. Delicious as an aperitif and with Asian dishes.

Keuka Spring Winery

280 Route 54
Penn Yan, NY 14527
(315) 536-3147
www.keukaspringwinery.com

Owners Len and Judy Wiltberger purchased a plot of land close to Keuka Lake from a neighbor 20 years ago and named it after a spring on the property. Today they are building a new winery and tasting room, where they will continue their focus on seyval blanc, vignoles, chardonnay, gewürztraminer, riesling, pinot noir, and Bordeaux varietals.

Keuka Spring Riesling 2004, Finger Lakes, New York, $14

Varietally expressive. A very high caliber wine. Good value.

Light-bodied, dry.

Apple, pear, lemongrass, Asian five-spice, gingerroot tea, and lanolin notes. Spicy and bright with tingly acidity and a mellow finish. Enjoy with seared salmon and bok choy, stir-fry, or fried chicken.

McGregor Vineyard

5503 Dutch Street
Dundee, NY 14837
(607) 292-3999
www.mcgregorwinery.com

Producing wine since 1980, the McGregor family follows the European or "Old World" model of winemaking, focusing not on winemaking techniques but rather the voice of the grape and its origin. Chardonnay, riesling, gewürztraminer, vignoles, muscat ottonel and pinot noir along with sereksia, saperavi, and rkazetili from Russia are the focus.

**McGregor Vineyard Semi-dry Riesling 2005,
Finger Lakes, New York, $20**

Distinctive style. Great for white zin fans as well as riesling fans.

Medium-bodied, off dry.

Candied violet, papaya, guava, and tropical notes with a sweet-tart, crisp finish. Enjoy with lemon chicken, grilled mahi mahi, or tempura.

Mountain Spirit Winery

8046 West U.S. Highway 50
Salida, CO 81201
(719) 539-7848
www.mountainspiritwinery.com

Located on five acres in Colorado's Upper Arkansas Valley and surrounded by fruit orchards, the Mountain Spirit Winery specializes in *vinifera*-fruit blends. The results are often surprisingly delicious—something different, as owner Terry Barkett and her co-vintner Mike Barkett say.

Mountain Spirit Riesling Blend (75% riesling, 25% chardonnay) 2003, Upper Arkansas River Valley, Colorado, $13

Unique blend.

Medium-bodied, off-dry.

Delicate aromas of stone-pit fruit, citrus, and toasty oak. Smooth and

lightly sweet, with juicy pear, peach and lemon zest notes, and a faintly oaky finish. Enjoy with prosciutto and melon or quiche.

Pey-Marin/Mount Tamalpais Vineyards

Post Office Box 912
San Anselmo, CA 94960
(415) 455-9463
www.marinwines.com

Jonathan and Susan Pey, proprietors, bring a wealth of premium wine experience in both France and California to the nascent Marin County wine industry. Mount Tamalpais is part of the Golden Gate National Recreation Area and is being recognized for cool-climate loving varietals riesling and pinot noir.

Pey-Marin Vineyards Riesling The Shell Mound 2005, Marin County, $20

First riesling and first screwcaps from Marin. Only 275 cases produced.

Light, dry.

This soft-spoken dry riesling has refreshing green apple notes and is delicious as an aperitif or lunchtime wine.

Piety Flats Winery

2560 Donald-Wapato Road
Wapato, WA 98951
(509) 877-3115
www.pietyflatswinery.com

In 2001, Partners Bryan Eglet and Jim Russi reopened Donald Fruit and Mercantile, which was originally opened in 1911, to serve as a general store. When they met Willow Crest's winemaker Dave Minick, the idea to turn the general store into Piety Flats Winery was born.

Piety Flats Riesling 2005, Yakima Valley, Washington, $12

Good example of Washington's riesling-making capability.

Light-bodied, off-dry.

Highly aromatic, with lush pear, peach, and floral notes. Zesty, tangy, citrusy, with a touch of pear, and a lively finish. Try it with fish tacos or a cool fruit salad.

Poet's Leap—Long Shadows

1604 Ireland Road
Walla Walla, WA 99362
(509) 526-0003
www.poetsleap.com

Founded by Allen Shoup, retired president of the Stimson Lane Wine Group, Long Shadows is a joint venture of several highly-acclaimed winemakers from around the world. Poet's Leap wines are crafted by Armin Diel, one of Germany's foremost riesling producers.

Poet's Leap Riesling 2004, Columbia Valley, Washington, $22

Exceptional wine from a German riesling specialist.

Light-bodied, dry.

Fresh floral and slightly minerally aromas with citrus accents. Notes of apricot, pineapple and rose petals, and a long, crisp finish. Excellent with oysters Rockefeller or sushi.

Rooster Hill Vineyards

489 Route 54 South
Penn Yan, NY 14527
(315) 536-4773
www.roosterhill.com

A Tuscan-style winery where the mood is relaxed, informal, and down to earth, Rooster Hill is managed by husband-and-wife team David and Amy Hoffman. Winemaker Barry Tortolon has a broad span of professional experience and has worked with such companies as Fulkerson Winery, Welch's Grape Juice, Fox Run Vineyards, and Glenora Wine Cellars.

Rooster Hill Estate Semi-Dry Riesling Savina and Catherine Vineyards 2005, Finger Lakes, New York, $16

The Finger Lakes are known for outstanding rieslings, and this is one of them.

Light-bodied, off-dry.

Lush fruity and floral aromas. Apricot, peach, citrus, and honey notes. Well balanced acids and sweetness. Delicious with honey chicken Dijon and summer squash.

Bokisch Ranches

18721 Cherry Road
Lodi, CA 95240
(209) 334-4338
www.bokischranches.com

This tiny artisanal winery specializes in Spanish varietal wines.
Owners Markus and Liz Bokisch lived and worked in Spain before
discovering this ranch in Lodi. They farm sustainably, harness solar
energy to power the wells, shop and house, and are phasing in
renewable biodiesel to replace petroleum-based diesel.

Bokisch Albarinho 2004, Lodi, $16

Best Albarinho in the USA.

Medium-bodied, dry.

Creamy and round with lemon, lime zest, and hazelnut notes.
Excellent with shrimp scampi, prawns and linguine, or seared scallops.

Silver Horse Vineyards

2995 Pleasant Road
San Miguel, CA 93451
(805) 467-WINE
www.silverhorse.com

The Kroener family operated Silver Horse Vineyard and Winery from a
converted barn from 1996 until 2005, when their new hilltop facility
was opened. They source most of their grapes from surrounding estate
vineyards and strive to make wines that winemaker Steve Kroener
describes as "100% food-friendly."

Silver Horse Albarino 2005, Edna Valley — San Luis Obispo, $24

Unforgettable nose. This rare American 100% albarino is topped by
a screwcap.

Light, dry.

Delicate aromas of white flowers and rose petals. Crisp and well
balanced, with apricot, peach, and floral notes. Enjoy with sushi and
Asian-inspired salads.

Casa Nuestra

3451 Silverado Trail North
St. Helena, CA 94574
(866) 844-WINE
www.casanuestra.com

Established in 1979, Casa Nuestra, or "Our House," produces about 1500 cases per year of cabernet sauvignon, cabernet franc, merlot, chenin blanc, riesling, and blends. Owner Gene Kirkham took over the property from his mother in 1974 and began learning about the pre-existing vines. He was joined by current chief winemaker Allen Price in the initial 1979 release.

Casa Nuestra Dry Chenin Blanc St. Helena Estate Home Vineyard 2005, Napa Valley, $24

A wonderfully expressive wine made from 40-year-old vines.

Medium-bodied, dry.

Bursting with green Jolly Rancher, peach, and toast notes. Notes of pineapple, banana, pear, and buttery oak, with an excellent balance of cleansing acids. Try it with halibut dijonaise topped with Parmesan cheese.

Kitfox Vineyards

1400 Rollins Road
Burlingame, CA 94010
(650) 342-3699
www.kitfoxvineyards.com

Fourth generation farmer Fred Vogel and his son, Hunter, replaced their almond, apricot, and walnut orchards with vines just outside of Patterson in 2000, then promptly submitted a petition for American Viticultural Area (AVA) status. The resulting Salado Creek AVA became official in August, 2004.

Kitfox Vineyards Foxy White 2004, California, $15

An aromatic blend with immediate appeal.

Light-bodied, dry.

This chenin-blanc based blend (it also has a little chardonnay, viognier, sauvignon blanc, and orange muscat) is musky and grapey with green apple, pear, pine, lanolin, and kiwi notes. Plump with underlying acidity for balance. Delicious as a cocktail, with orange-maple marinated shrimp skewers, or with jalapeño chicken taquitos.

Wilson Vineyards

50400 Gaffney Road
Post Office Box 307
Clarksburg, CA 95612
(916) 744-1456
www.wilsonvineyards.com

Now in their third generation, the Wilson family vineyards are under the stewardship of Ken, who sells some of the fruit to big name as well as cult California producers. His sister Sandra is in charge of marketing.

Wilson Vineyards Chenin Blanc-Viognier 2003, Clarksburg, $9

Good value.

Medium-bodied, dry.

Peach, kiwi, lanolin, hay, and toasted almond notes. Silky center with candied notes and a sweet-tart pineapple finish. Delicious with Gruyère-stuffed mushroom caps or with a melon-curry salad.

Domenico Wines

1697 Industrial Road
San Carlos, CA 94070
(650) 593-2335
www.domenicowines.com

Cal-Ital, or California-Italian varietals, are the specialty of this small
winery, including pinot grigio, sangiovese, and barbera. These are
wines to enjoy everyday at the table.

Domenico Pinot Grigio 2004, Lodi, $18

Pure, unadulterated varietal expression from healthy vines.

Medium-bodied, dry.

Clean, brisk, tart, and pithy (think inside the lemon skin) with dill,
lemon, and a sweet tart/cherimoya/tropical edge, a soft, supple piney
core, and a long peachy, piney, lemony finish. Especially delicious with
prosciutto-wrapped breadsticks.

Margerum Wine Company

2556 Franceschi Road
Santa Barbara, CA 93103
(805) 892-9711
www.margerumwinecompany.com

Throughout his 20 years in the wine industry, Doug Margerum always
dreamed of having a winery small enough that he could run it mostly
by himself. At 240 square feet—smaller than an average garage—
his is the smallest bonded winery in Santa Barbara County.

Margerum Pinot Gris Alisos Vineyards 2005, Santa Barbara County, $18

Margerum's benchmark white wine for 2005. 284 cases produced.

Medium-bodied, dry.

Deliciously aromatic, with green apple, peach, and citrus notes. The
palate is zesty and smooth with juicy citrus and peach notes and a
slight mineral tone. Try it with a summery Asian salad of shrimp,
jicama, papaya, and ginger vinaigrette.

41

Midlife Crisis Winery

1244 Pine Street, Suite A
Paso Robles, CA 93446
(805) 237-8730
www.midlifecrisiswinery.com

Midlife Crisis Winery is fully owned and operated by Kevin and Jill
Mittan. After years of making wine in their garage in Los Angeles, the
Mittans sold their L.A. home and bought 22 acres of prime vineyard
land in Paso Robles. September 2004 was their first crush.

Midlife Crisis Pinot Grigio 2004, Paso Robles, $16.50

Warm climate, fruit-forward expression of the varietal.

Medium-bodied, dry.

Aromas of tropical fruit, peach, and vanilla. Zesty and tangy, with a
lemony, buttery, pineapple and green apple flavors, and firm acidity.
Pairs well with sesame-seed encrusted ahi tuna with plum sauce, or
serve alone as an aperitif.

Banyan Wines

10295 Westside Road
Healdsburg, CA 95448
(707) 887-0833
www.banyanwines.com

Father and son Somchai and Kenny Likitprakong of Thailand own and
operate this small winery whose focus is "appellation specific wines
that pair with Asian cuisines."

Banyan Gewürztraminer 2005, Monterey County, $10

One of the best in the U.S. Excellent Value. 469 cases produced.

Medium-bodied, dry.

Buttercream, lychee, rose water, tangerine, mandarin orange, guava,
key lime and peach notes with a lively, pithy, and very slightly sweet
finish. Built for spicy Chinese or Thai dishes.

Broad Run Vineyards

10601 Broad Run Road
Louisville, KY 40299
(502) 231-0372
www.broadrunvineyards.com

Broad Run Vineyards began in 1983 as an experiment to see what
varietals would grow well in Kentucky soil. Pleased with the results,
the Kushner-Hyatt family went commercial in 1992, releasing their first
vintage in 1994. Broad Run was officially bonded in 2003. All their
grapes are estate-grown.

**Broad Run Gewürztraminer 2002, Ohio River
Valley, Kentucky, $16**

A good example of Kentucky's gewürztraminer-making capabilities.

Light-bodied, dry.

Lush floral and citrus aromas. Tangy on the palate, with notes of
crushed rose petals, lychee, and toasty oak, leading into a long,
slightly spicy finish. Delicious with smoked oysters, or try it with
macaroni and cheese.

Harvest Moon Winery

2192 Olivet Road
Santa Rosa, CA 95401
(707) 573-8711
www.harvestmoonwinery.com

Proprietors Bob and Ginny Pitts released their first wine in 2002. While they specialize in zinfandel from their 11-acre plot in the Russian River Valley, they also produce a limited amount of gewürztraminer and pinot noir, as well as olive oil. Son Randy Pitts is winemaker.

Harvest Moon Gewürztraminer Brut 2003, Russian River Valley, $24

America's best sparkling gewürztraminer. Made from 30-year-old vines.

Medium-bodied, off dry, sparkling.

Light and delicate lychee, floral, and green apple notes. Clean fresh lime zest/honey finish. Enjoy as an aperitif, with brunch, or with a picnic. Delicious with lobster or freshly cracked crab.

Keuka Spring Winery

280 Route 54
Penn Yan, NY 14527
(315) 536-3147
www.keukaspringwinery.com

Owners Len and Judy Wiltberger purchased a plot of land close to Keuka Lake from a neighbor 20 years ago and named it after a spring on the property. Today they are building a new winery and tasting room, where they will continue their focus on seyval blanc, vignoles, chardonnay, gewürztraminer, riesling, pinot noir, and Bordeaux varietals.

Keuka Spring Gewurztraminer 2004, Finger Lakes, New York, $15

Pristine varietal expression. Good value.

Medium-bodied, dry.

Lanolin, candlewax, yellow and pink rose, apple, pear, peach, and caramelized banana notes. Very soft and luscious with balanced acids and a long, peachy/hazelnut/mineral finish. Enjoy with hoisin barbecued chicken, chicken liver pâté, or Camembert cheese.

Stony Hill

Post Office Box 308
St. Helena, CA 94574
(707) 963-2636
www.stonyhillvineyard.com

In 1943, Fred and Eleanor McCrea bought a 160-acre goat ranch on the northeast slope of Spring Mountain and began planting vineyards in 1947. Theirs was the first winery built in the Napa Valley (in 1952) after prohibition. Assisted by long-time winemaker Mike Chelini and the Roque, Salomon, and Rodriquez families who for generations have worked in the vineyard, the McCrea family continues to focus on dry, steely chardonnay, semillon, white riesling, and gewürztraminer.

Stony Hill Gewürztraminer 2004, Napa Valley, $13.50

Unique style. Good value.

Medium-bodied, dry.

Delicate notes of lychee, pink grapefruit, lemon, and lime with rich, vibrant acidity. Delicious with fish, chicken or tofu with lychee barbecue sauce, or with Chef Nam Phan's (Napa General Store) Crispy Crabmeat and Pork Springroll with Ginger Dipping Sauce.

Arger-Martucci Vineyards

1455 Inglewood Avenue
St. Helena, CA 94574
(707) 963-4334
www.arger-martucci.com

In 1998, Rich and Carol Martucci and Julie and Kosta Arger partnered to produce small, handcrafted lots of red, white, and dessert wines. Rich and Carol's son Vincent is winemaker. Kosta and Julie's daughter Katarena oversees sales and marketing as well as hospitality.

Arger-Martucci Viognier 2005, Russian River Valley, $25

At 26 years, these viognier vines are some of the oldest in America. 390 cases produced.

Full-bodied, dry.

Clean and refreshing with white rose, peach, almond, and lanolin notes. Silky and smooth. Enjoy with shrimp Louie, or honey-ginger marinated chicken or tofu.

Banyan Wines

10295 Westside Road
Healdsburg, CA 95448
(707) 887-0833
www.banyanwines.com

Father and son Somchai and Kenny Likitprakong of Thailand own and operate this small winery whose focus is "appellation specific wines that pair with Asian cuisines."

Banyan Viognier 2005, Madera, $15

Good value.

Medium-bodied, dry.

Lemon pot du crème, peach, pineapple, marzipan, cognac, and toffee notes. Warm and round with a clean, dry finish. Enjoy with chicken satay or macadamia-dipped tempeh with bamboo rice.

Brennan Vineyards

802 South Austin Street
Post Office Box 399
Comanche, Texas 76442
(325) 356-9100
www.brennanvineyards.com

Owned by the Brennan family, Brennan Vineyards is located in the
McCrary House in Comanche, Texas, a limestone house built in 1879.
They purchased the property in 1997 and decided shortly thereafter
to grow grapes on 33 adjacent acres. Together with the Wilkerson
family, they are celebrating their first release this year.

Brennan Viognier 2005, Texas Hill Country, Texas, $15

Considering the challenging viticultural conditions in Texas, this is
quite an accomplishment.

Medium-bodied, dry.

Fruity aromas with delicate floral undertones. Peach, citrus, rose, and
green pea notes. Smooth and creamy on the palate, with a fresh
finish. Great with raw vegetables and ranch dip, or try it with a
spinach and mushroom omelet.

Carina Cellars

2900 Grand Avenue, Suite A
Los Olivos, CA 93441
(805) 688-2459
www.carinacellars.com

Carina Cellars is the result of a fruitful meeting between attorney and
businessman David Hardee and winemaker Joey Tensley of Tensely
Wine Company in 2002. After combining their efforts, the team
produced their first release of syrah and cabernet sauvignon in 2004.

Carina Cellars Viognier 2005, Central Coast, $22

One of the top viogniers from the Central Coast.

Medium-bodied, dry.

Aromas of pineapples, mangoes, pears, and kiwi. Floral and tropical fruit notes, followed by a zesty, lemony finish. Excellent with grilled shrimp and pineapple skewers.

Clautiere Vineyard

1340 Penman Springs Road
Paso Robles, CA 93446
(805) 237-3789
www.clautiere.com

Owners Claudine Blackwell and Terry Brady, whose combined backgrounds include experience in dining, fashion designing, and welding, have described the winery they opened in 1999 as "A winery...where Edward Scissorhands meets the Mad Hatter at the Moulin Rouge."

Clautiere Viognier Estate Grown 2004, Paso Robles, $23

Beautifully balanced.

Medium-bodied, dry.

Tropical fruit aromas of pineapple, banana, and honey. Juicy and tangy, with notes of apricot, pineapple, peach and pear, and a crisp, fresh finish. Delicious with lightly spiced seafood appetizers such as shrimp cocktail or ceviche.

Dover Canyon Winery

4520 Vineyard Drive
Paso Robles, CA 93446
(805) 237-0101
www.dovercanyon.com

Owner and winemaker Dan Panico, former winemaker for Eberle Winery, has been making wine for 17 years. He started producing his own in 1992 while still at Eberle. Mary Baker, former director of the Paso Robles Wine Country Alliance, does marketing and helps on the crush pad and in the vineyard. Dover Canyon is a certified wildlife habitat.

Dover Canyon Viognier Hansen Vineyard 2004, Paso Robles, $22

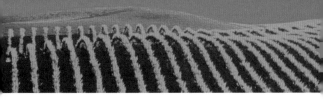

Lush expression of the varietal. 190 cases produced.

Medium-bodied, dry.

Richly perfumed with floral and mineral notes. Bursting with tropical fruit and peach flavors. Creamy, buttery finish. Enjoy with Thai food, or try it with fried catfish and hush puppies.

Fralich Vineyard & Winery

6305 Buena Vista Drive, Suite P4
Paso Robles, CA 93446
(805) 434-1526
www.fralichvineyard.com

Owner and winemaker Harry Fralich bought his 20-acre property outside Templeton in 1980. In 1992, he began planting the Spanish and Portuguese varietals in which he now specializes. He sells 80% of his grapes and keeps the rest to produce about 1000 cases each year.

Fralich Viognier 2004, Paso Robles, $26

Warm climate, fruit-forward style.

Medium-bodied, dry.

Delicate aromas of pear, pineapple, and rose petals. Creamy, floral palate, with rose, pear and melon notes, and a clean, lingering finish. Delicious with sautéed red snapper and wild rice.

Frick Winery

23072 Walling Road
Geyserville, CA 95441
(707) 857-1980
www.frickwinery.com

Husband and wife team Judith Gannon and Bill Frick founded their Dry Creek Valley winery in 1976 with the proceeds of their beloved 1957 Chevy and after emptying both of their savings accounts. Today they produce 1800 cases total, of syrah, merlot, cinsault, and viognier using sustainable farming and artisanal production methods.

Frick Viognier Gannon Vineyard 2003, Dry Creek Valley, $25

Many California viogniers lose their delicate perfume in the warm sun and then are overoaked. This wine is the exception to the rule.

Medium-bodied, dry.

Pretty floral and peach notes with a bold, spicy, tingly palate, and a slightly bitter finish. Enjoy with Camembert or Brie cheese with dried apricots and walnut bread.

JM Cellars

14404 137th Place Northeast
Woodinville, WA 98072
(206) 321-0052
www.jmcellars.com

JM Cellars is a family-owned winery located on the "Bramble Bump," just above Chateau St. Michelle in Woodinville, Washington. Owner and winemaker John Bigelow learned from one of the best—Mike Januik of Januik winery.

JM Cellars Viognier 2005, Columbia Valley, Washington, $22

Beautifully aromatic and expressive.

Medium-bodied, dry.

Aromas of apricot, peach, and citrus. Luscious peach, citrus, and oak notes, with a long, crisp finish. Try it with freshly grilled salmon or crab enchiladas.

Keswick Vineyards

1575 Keswick Winery Drive
Keswick, VA 22947
(434) 244-3341
www.keswickvineyards.com

Located at the 400-acre Edgewood Estate which was part of the 1727 Nicholas Meriwether Crown Grant, Keswick Vineyards is owned by Al and Cindy Schornberg. Michael Shaps, formerly of Jefferson Vineyards, joined the Schornbergs in 2002 as the consulting winemaker.

Keswick Viognier Les Vents d'Anges 2004, Monticello, Virginia, $17

Lean style.

Medium-bodied, dry.

Fruity aromas, with flavors of apricot and peach, and fine oak tannins. Crisp, lingering finish. Delicious with lobster salad and toasted baguette slices.

Alexandria Nicole Cellars

2880 Lee Road
Prosser, Washington 99350
(509) 786-3497
www.alexandrianicolecellars.com

On the bluffs overlooking the Columbia River in Washington State, former Assistant Viticulturalist for Hogue Cellars, Jarrod Boyle planted the first vines of his estate vineyard, Destiny Ridge, in 1998. He then went on to found Alexandria Nicole Cellars, where he produces about 4800 cases a year of 15 different varietals.

Alexandria Nicole Viognier Reserve Destiny Ridge Vineyards 2005, Columbia Valley, Washington, $18

An exceptionally well balanced viognier. Great value.

Light-bodied, dry.

Very fragrant, fruity nose of pineapple and apricot notes. Well balanced and complex, with tropical fruit, melon, citrus and floral notes, and a clean finish. Enjoy with chicken saltimbocca.

Chateau de Deighton Winery

2515 Lara Lane
Oceano, CA 93445
(805) 489-0979
www.chateaudedeighton.com

Computer engineer, humorist, and winery owner Mark Hutchenreuther
makes his wine at Paso Roble Wine Services, a custom crush facility
in Paso Robles. He sources grapes from Herder Vineyard, French Camp
Vineyard, and Scheid Vineyard, among others.

Chateau de Deighton Cuvee Blanc (semillon/ sauvignon blanc) 2004, Central Coast, $10

Beautifully balanced. Excellent value.

Light-bodied, dry.

Zesty and fruity, with aromas of pineapple, banana, and peach.
Buttery oak, melon, and pineapple notes, with a vibrant finish.
Try it with grilled orange roughy topped with lemon zest.

Broman Cellars

945 Deer Park Road
St. Helena, CA 94574
(800) 514-4401
www.bromancellars.com

Owner and winemaker Bob Broman worked with Stag's Leap Wine
Cellars, Concannon Vineyards, St. Supery, and Guenoc before launching
his owner label in 1994. He produces a cabernet sauvignon, sauvignon
blanc, and syrah.

Broman Sauvignon Blanc 2003, Napa Valley, $16

Tart style unusual for Napa Valley. 300 cases made.

Medium-bodied, dry.

Clean lemon, mango, and grassy notes. Vivacious natural acidity and
a crisp finish. Enjoy with oysters on the half shell or a lobster roll with
corn on the cob.

Flying Horse Winery

2825 St. Helena Highway North
St. Helena, CA 94574
(888) 294-2776
www.flyinghorsewines.com

Owner Bryant Morris, creator of Raging Waters and many other
famous water parks in the U.S., who also magnificently restores
carousel horses, thus the name, is now restoring Pope Valley's Aetna
Springs resort. He planted 24 acres of vineyards with sauvignon blanc,
cabernet sauvignon, and petite sirah. Jennifer Rue is winemaker, and
Joshua Clark is vineyard manager.

Flying Horse Sauvignon Blanc 2004, Napa
Valley, $23

More flavorful than a typical Napa Valley sauvignon blanc.
300 cases produced.

Medium-bodied, dry.

Gooseberry, papaya, key lime, and canned pea notes with a zesty, lemony finish. Bold and rich. Delicious with spicy cuisine or seafood.

Halleck Vineyards

3785 Burnside Road
Sebastopol, CA 95472
(707) 738-8383
www.halleckvineyards.com

Ross Halleck and his wife Jennifer still have one foot in their previous careers (Ross is founder of Halleck Design Group) while they launch their own small winery. Their one-acre site, intended to serve as a college fund for their three sons, is turning out to produce phenomenal sauvignon blanc, gewürztraminer, and pinot noir. Winemaker Greg Lafollette, formerly of Flowers, vineyard manager Eric Neal, and vineyard consultant Greg Bjornstad roundout the team.

Halleck Vineyard Sauvignon Blanc Piner Creek Ranch 2004, Russian River Valley, $28

Sancerre meets San Tropez. 338 cases produced.

Full-bodied, dry.

Gooseberry, lemon, key lime pie, apple pie, nutmeg, and zesty pink grapefruit notes. Decadently fruity with a silky palate and vibrant, juicy, natural acidity. Enjoy with Asian noodles with chili shrimp and cashews, or crab quesadillas with mango salsa.

Hunnicutt

1860 Howell Mountain Road
St. Helena, CA 94574
(707) 963-2908
www.drstephenswines.com

Justin Hunnicutt Stephens, son of D.R. Stephens Estate Wines founder and proprietor Don Stephens, left his career in commercial real estate to work in the wine business. Starting from the ground up, he worked at Miner Vineyards, Saddleback Cellars, and Seavey Vineyards before

joining the family business in 2004. He is now general manager for both D.R. Stephens and his own label, Hunnicutt.

Hunnicutt Sauvignon Blanc 2005, Pope Valley—Napa Valley, $19

Good value. 198 cases produced.

Medium-bodied, dry.

Tropical, melon, honey, and peach notes. Rich and vibrant with a clean finish. Enjoy as an aperitif, with a chilled seafood platter, or with jerk chicken.

Margerum Wine Company

2556 Franceschi Road
Santa Barbara, CA 93103
(805) 892-9711
www.margerumwinecompany.com

Throughout his 20 years in the wine industry, Doug Margerum always dreamed of having a winery small enough that he could run it mostly by himself. At 240 square feet—smaller than an average garage—his is the smallest bonded winery in Santa Barbara County.

Margerum Sauvignon Blanc Vogelzang Vineyard 2005, Santa Ynez Valley—Santa Barbara, $20

Well-crafted. Good value.

Medium-bodied, dry.

Zesty and tangy, with citrus, melon and slight grassy notes, and a long, crisp finish. Excellent with grilled red snapper and fresh baby peas.

Raphael

39390 Main Road (Route 25)
Post Office Box 17
Peconic, NY 11958
(631) 765-1100
www.raphaelwine.com

John Petrocelli established this winery in 1996 and named it after his father. The 60-acre vineyard is located on a gentle slope overlooking the Peconic Bay, just 2000 feet away. Looking to the great Bordeaux wines for inspiration, Petrocelli hired consulting enologist Paul Pontallier, of Chateau Margaux. Sustainable farming and hand harvesting are practiced.

Raphael Sauvignon Blanc 2005, North Fork of Long Island, $22

A fine example of the varietal.

Medium-bodied, dry.

Pink grapefruit, lime zest, peach, kiwi, mango, and peppermint notes. Soft, silky texture. Zippy. Delicious with Mediterranean appetizers like taramosalata, tzatziki (cucumber yogurt sauce) with keftedes (spiced meatballs), or a seafood platter.

Shannon Ridge

12599 East Highway 20
Clearlake Oaks, CA 95423
(707) 998-9656
www.shannonridge.com

Owners Clay and Margarita Shannon met while working at the same Napa winery. In 1995, they visited a property perched atop a steep mountain ridge about 35 miles north of the Napa county line. Cooled by winds off of nearby Clear Lake, and with lean, volcanic soils, the couple knew they were home. Vineyard Manager Celestino Castañeda and winemaker Marco DiGiulio oversee the growing and production of zinfandel, cabernet sauvignon, barbera, petite sirah, and sauvignon blanc from this rugged site.

Shannon Ridge Sauvignon Blanc 2004, Lake County, $15

A lively, varietally expressive style unencumbered by oak.

Medium-bodied, dry.

Pink grapefruit, key lime, and spring asparagus notes on a fresh peachy palate with a zesty green bean finish. Clay and Margarita recommend this with turkey, bacon, and spinach wraps.

Work Vineyard

3190 Highway 128
Calistoga, CA 94515
(707) 942-0251
www.workvineyard.com

Karen and Henry Work moved to Napa Valley from San Diego in 1974, and immersed themselves in the wine business. In 1987, they purchased a three-acre sauvignon blanc vineyard in Calistoga and became grape growers, selling to Caymus and Cakebread, amongst others. In 2001, they launched their own label with a 230 case production and today produce about 1200 cases. Sustainable farming is practiced.

Work Vineyard Sauvignon Blanc 2005, Napa Valley, $24.50

A crisp, refreshing New Zealand style.

Medium-bodied, dry.

Fresh cut grass, asparagus, lemon zest, and pink grapefruit notes with a sweet-tart lemon lime aftertaste. Enjoy as an aperitif alone or with crème de cassis as a kir, or with goat cheese and crusty sourdough bread.

Alfaro Family Vineyards & Winery

496 Hames Road
Corralitos, CA 95076
(831) 728-5172
www.alfarowine.com

Owners Richard and Mary Kay Alfaro work solely towards producing Burgundian varietals chardonnay and pinot noir from their estate vineyards in the Santa Cruz Mountains.

Alfaro Family Vineyards Chardonnay 2004, Santa Cruz Mountains, $25

Rich, buttery style with restrained fruit.

Full-bodied, dry.

Honey, butter, peach, crème caramel, and toasty oak notes. Very buttery with juicy acidity and an oaky finish. Enjoy as a cocktail or with lobster with drawn butter.

Martin Alfaro

496 Hames Road
Corralitos, CA 95076
(831) 728-5172
www.martinalfaro.com

The partnership of Richard Alfaro, a former artisanal baker, and wine industry veteran Joseph Martin, who worked with Richard Graff, focuses on Burgundian style chardonnay and pinot noir along with merlot, cabernet sauvignon, and zinfandel from their 30 acres of vineyards in the Santa Cruz Mountains.

Martin Alfaro Chardonnay 2004, Santa Cruz Mountains, $18

Excellent value.

Full-bodied, dry.

Peach, banana, crème brûlée and toasted almond, and caramel notes. Big and bold with a silky middle. Balanced with a crisp aftertaste. Delicious with fresh cracked crab, butternut squash risotto, or butternut squash quinoa pilaf.

Arcadian Winery

Post Office Box 1395
Santa Ynez, CA 93460
(805) 452-7413
www.arcadianwinery.com

Winemaker Joe Davis fell in love with the world of wine while in college after tasting Domaine Dujac's Clos de la Roche, one of the best Burgundies (pinot noirs) in the world. In 1985, he started working for Dan Lee of Morgan Winery and then moved on to Bernardus Winery where he was general manager. He released Arcadian Winery's first vintage in 1996.

Arcadian Chardonnay Sleepy Hollow Vineyards 2002, Santa Lucia Highlands—Monterey County, $35

Excellent expression of the Sleepy Hollow Vineyards, one America's top sources of chardonnay.

Medium-bodied, dry.

Initial flavors of white flowers, melon, and kiwi, followed by lemon zest, and tropical fruit notes. Complex and well balanced, with medium acids. Pairs well with lobster Newburg or cracked crab salad.

Clos Pepe Vineyards and Estate Wines

4777 East Highway 246
Lompoc, CA 93436
(805) 735-2196
www.clospepe.com

Wes Hagen, a regular judge, along with author Catherine Fallis, at the Los Angeles County Fair, introduced her to his wines, and to the pending legislation for Santa Barbara's newest American Viticultural Area (AVA), the Santa Rita Hills a few years back. Wes, his mother, wife, and father-in-law Steve Pepe oversee every aspect of the business. The Hagens employ sustainable farming.

Clos Pepe Estate Chardonnay "Homage to Chablis" 2004, Santa Rita Hills, $25

This chardonnay is the antithesis of the popular ripe fruit, sweet oak, and buttery style.

Full-bodied, dry.

Intensely minerally and rich, this broad-shouldered wine is more like a Chateauneuf-du-Pape blanc, a big white from France's Rhone Valley, than a California chardonnay. Slightly mysterious with lurking flavors that are hard to pin down. Delicious with oysters, sushi, or cows milk cheeses such as Babybel, Brie, Emmentaler, or Taleggio.

Cooper Vineyards

13372 Shannon Hill Road
Louisa, VA 23093
(804) 285-7533
www.coopervineyards.com

Located on 36 acres in Central Virginia, Cooper Vineyards was founded in 1999 by current owners Geoffery Cooper and Jacqueline Hogge. Winemaker Graham Bell has over 20 years' experience and produces handcrafted wine from several varietals, including their specialty, the native Virginian norton grape.

Cooper Vineyards White Blend Coopertage Blanc multi-vintage, Virginia, $15

An excellent white blend combining chardonnay's elegance with viognier's sweet perfume.

Medium-bodied, dry.

With aromas of honey, citrus, and French oak, this 80% chardonnay/ 20% viognier blend is well balanced. Honey, vanilla, lemon, and orange blossom notes, and a soft, buttery finish. Great with Asian-fusion-style shrimp salad.

Corey Creek Vineyards/Bedell North Fork LLC

36225 Main Road (Route 25)
Cutchogue, NY 11935
(631) 765-4168
www.bedellcellars.com

Owner Michael Lynne, Co-Chairman and Co-CEO of New Line Cinema, met founding winemaker Kip Bedell who had established the seven-acre Bedell Vineyards at the site of an old potato farm. He now oversees the 78-acre property along with winemaker John Irving Levenberg. Vineyard Manager Dave Thompson is a member of the board of the Long Island Sustainable Agriculture program.

Corey Creek Vineyards Chardonnay 2004, North Fork of Long Island, New York, $18

Incredible balance of decadent fruit and cleansing acids.

Medium-bodied, dry.

Caramel apple, nilla wafer, crème brûlée, and lemony notes. Round, creamy, and buttery with well-integrated oak and a clean, refreshingly tart finish. Delicious with veal blanquette, chicken Cordon Bleu, or Lean Cuisine chicken pasta selection.

Devitt

11412 Highway 238
Applegate, OR 97530
(541) 899-7511
www.devittwinery.com

After having owned Pope Valley Winery in Napa Valley for 15 years, owner and winemaker James Devitt took a hiatus from the wine business in the mid-1980s. He returned and opened Devitt in 2001, focusing mostly on red varietals, as well as viognier, and chardonnay.

Devitt Chardonnay 2003, Applegate Valley, Oregon, $16

Excellent value. One of the few quality Oregon chardonnays at this price point.

Full-bodied, dry.

Fruity aromas of pear, citrus, lychee, and oak. Fresh and tingly on the palate, with pear, grapefruit, and oak notes and a long finish. Enjoy with fish and chips or baked haddock.

Hanzell Vineyards

18596 Lomita Avenue
Sonoma, CA 95476
(707) 996-3860
www.hanzell.com

Hanzell is an icon. In 1948, Ambassador James D. Zellerbach acquired this 200-acre estate in the Mayacamas Mountains. In 1953, six acres was planted to pinot noir in 1953 (this is America's oldest pinot noir vineyard). Current owner Alexander de Brye and his family continue the tradition of crafting Burgundian style (elegant, understated, and minerally wines) today. Three quarters of the production is chardonnay.

Hanzell Vineyards Chardonnay 2003, Sonoma Valley, $65

One of America's most ageworthy white wines, and a serious competitor of French white Burgundy at twice the price.

Full-bodied, dry.

This steely, dry wine is not forthcoming, nor is it immediately appealing. It opens slowly in the glass, revealing its personality layer by layer, sip by sip. It is a splurge, so delicate, subtly flavored dishes are best. Think salmon en brioche, scrambled eggs with truffle oil, or, if Bill Gates is paying, a fresh black truffle and butter sandwich.

Heringer Estates

37375 Netherlands Road
Clarksburg, CA 95612
(916) 302-7095
www.heringerestates.com

With five generations in the farming business, the Heringer family has access to some of the finest vineyards in this underdog wine growing area. Petite sirah was their first release, in 2004, though Clarksburg is renowned for both chardonnay and chenin blanc.

Heringer Estates Chardonnay 2004, Clarksburg, $13

Excellent value. Be the first kid on the block to "discover" it.

Medium-bodied, dry.

Crowd-pleasing creamy style with vivid Jolly Rancher green apple, strawberry galette, butter cream, and light toasty notes. Excellent for entertaining, and delicious with roasted chicken and German potato salad, or with sesame chicken.

Hunter Wine Cellars

Post Office Box 561
Sebastopol, CA 95473
(707) 829-1941
www.chasseurwines.com

After working with Rombauer, Bonny Doon, and others, Bill Hunter started making his own wine in Sonoma. So impressed with the 1999 Hunter Wine Cellar releases, Alex Bartholomaus, owner of Billington Imports, offered to invest in the business and became a minority partner. Bill selected the name "Chasseur," French for "hunter," as the brand name for his wines.

Chasseur Chardonnay 2004, Russian River Valley, $35

A deft blend of bold California fruit with French elegance.

Full-bodied, dry. 429 cases produced.

This luscious, creamy wine has brown sugar-glazed roasted pineapple notes with buttered toast, hazelnuts, and bright acid on the palate and a long, buttery/nutty finish. Delicious with butternut squash and sage ravioli or sea bass with cream sauce.

Jack Creek Cellars

5265 Jack Creek Road
Templeton, CA 93465
(805) 226-8283
www.jackcreekcellars.com

Jack Creek Cellars exemplifies the spirit of a boutique winery. Dedicated to growing grapes of the highest quality, owners Doug and Sabrina Kruse focus on producing a small quantity of unfiltered artisan wines each year.

Jack Creek Chardonnay 2004, York Mountain, $28

Beautifully balanced. Well crafted.

Medium-bodied, dry.

Sweet and buttery, with aromas of melon and citrus. Delicately balanced citrus, melon, lychee, and toasted oak notes. Crisp, lingering finish. Delicious with mushroom risotto.

Naked Mountain Vineyard

2747 Leeds Manor Road
Post Office Box 115
Markham, VA 22643
(540) 364-1609
www.nakedmtn.com

Bob and Phoebe Harper were amateur winemakers for years before they bought some property in the Blue Ridge Mountains of Virginia and planted their own *vinifera* grapes in 1976. Though they had intended for the vineyard to be just a hobby, it quickly grew into a commercial venture. The winery, established in 1981, now produces about 5000 cases per year of vinifera table wines, specializing in chardonnay.

Naked Mountain Chardonnay 2002, Virginia, $17

Benchmark wine for Naked Mountain.

Medium-bodied, dry.

Aromas of toast, pear, and citrus. Well balanced and smooth, with pear, papaya, toasty oak, and butterscotch notes. Try it with macadamia-encrusted mahi-mahi, or enjoy with Southern fried chicken and potato chips.

Oak Mountain Winery

36522 Via Verde
Temecula, CA 92592
(951) 699-9102
www.oakmountainwinery.com

Steve and Valerie Andrews opened Oak Mountain, the sister winery to Temecula Hills Winery, in 2001. Situated atop a ridge, the winery produces limited quantities of cabernet sauvignon, merlot, petite verdot, cabernet franc, malbec, mourvedre, and primitivo. Steve is the winemaker, while Valerie manages the business side of things.

Oak Mountain Chardonnay Weaver Vineyard 2005, Temecula Valley, $18

Good effort for Temecula.

Medium-bodied, dry.

Zesty and lemony, with several layers of citrus and undertones of apple, melon, and green peas. The finish is long and creamy, with faint oak notes. Delicious with stuffed clams or shrimp scampi.

O'Brien Family Vineyard

Oak Knoll District
Napa, CA 94558
(707) 252-8463
www.obrienfamilyvineyard.com

In March of 2000, Bart and Barb O'Brien purchased the former Costello Winery in the Oak Knoll District of Napa Valley. With the help of vineyard and cellar manager Michael Hanna, the great-great-grandson of John Muir, winemaker Dave Cofran formerly of Silver Oak Cellars, and consulting winemaker Hugh Chappelle (Flowers Vineyards and currently with Lynmar), they produce chardonnay, merlot, and a Bordeaux blend.

O'Brien Family Vineyard "O" Chardonnay 2004, Napa Valley, $20

Decadent, super-rich style.

Full-bodied, dry.

Apple, pear, peach cobbler, crème brûlée, caramel, butterscotch, and honey notes. Big, buttery, oaky style. Enjoy as a cocktail.

Pearmund Cellars

6190 Georgetown Road
Broad Run, VA 20137
(540) 347-3475
www.pearmundcellars.com

After 12 years as the owner of Meriweather Winery, owner and wine-maker Chris Pearmund established Pearmund Cellars—a 7,500 square foot geothermal winery—in 2003. They now produce about 5000 cases per year of chardonnay, viognier, riesling, cabernet franc, and many other varietals.

Pearmund Cellars Estate Chardonnay 2004, Virginia, $19

A crowd-pleaser.

Medium-bodied, dry.

Tangy citrus, tart green apple, and toasty oak notes. Lime and pear notes on the finish. Delicious with a Chinese chicken salad with orange sesame seed dressing.

Peters Family Winery

2064 Highway 116 North, Suite 102
Sebastopol, CA 95472
(707) 829-3111
www.petersfamilywinery.com

Owner and winemaker Douglas M. Peters crafts site specific, unfiltered wines in the European style.

Peters Family Winery Chardonnay Sangiocomo Vineyard 2003, Carneros—Sonoma, $34

A Burgundian style that reflects its single vineyard origin.
214 cases produced.

Medium-bodied, dry.

Dusty, butter, bosc pear, and apple tart notes. Firm acidity. Built for the table. Enjoy with grilled chicken, almond crusted fillet of sole, or bay scallops in puff pastry with lobster cream sauce.

Rooster Hill Vineyards

489 Route 54 South
Penn Yan, NY 14527
(315) 536-4773
www.roosterhill.com

A Tuscan-style winery where the mood is relaxed, informal, and down to earth, Rooster Hill is managed by husband-and-wife team David and Amy Hoffman. Winemaker Barry Tortolon has a broad span of professional experience and has worked with such companies as Fulkerson Winery, Welch's Grape Juice, Fox Run Vineyards, and Glenora Wine Cellars.

Rooster Hill Chardonnay 2005, Finger Lakes, New York, $14

Good value.

Medium-bodied, dry.

Notes of pear, vanilla, and hazelnut on the nose. Creamy and supple, with honey, spice, and oak tones and a lemony finish. Excellent with a grilled chicken Caesar salad.

Rosenthal — The Malibu Estate

29000 Newton Canyon Road
Malibu, CA 90265
(310) 463-9532
www.rosenthalestatewines.com

George Rosenthal planted vineyards at his 250-acre Malibu estate in 1987, after having owned hotels and movies studios for a number of years. Winemaker is Christian Roguenant, whose credits include a stint as winemaker and president of Laetitia Winery.

Rosenthal Chardonnay 2004, Malibu Newton Canyon, $22.50

Excellent vintage for Malibu Newton Canyon.

Medium-bodied, dry.

Creamy and zesty, with green apple, pear, citrus, and vanilla notes. Well balanced acids and judicious oak use. Long, fresh finish. Try it with Thai coconut chicken or breaded shrimp.

Roudon Smith Winery

2364 Bean Creek Road
Scotts Valley, CA 95066
(831) 438-1244
www.roudonsmith.com

Bob Roudon and Jim Smith, two Silicon Valley engineers who made their career changes in 1972, recently retired and sold the winery to the Hunt family. Owner and operator David Hunt continues to focus on estate chardonnay, cabernet sauvignon from Monterey, and pinot noir and chardonnay from the Russian River Valley.

Roudon Smith Chardonnay Estate 2004, Santa Cruz Mountains, $22

A rare find with so little actual vineyard area left in this appellation. Good Value.

Full-bodied, dry.

Butterscotch, mango, and vanilla notes. Rich and decadent style. Very creamy with an underlying note of ginger ale for balance. Delicious with pumpkin or oyster bisque, or poached scallops Mornay.

RustRidge Vineyard & Winery

2910 Lower Chiles Valley Road
St. Helena, CA 94574
(707) 965-9353
www.rustridge.com

Owners Jim Fresquez and Susan Meyer took over RustRidge Ranch in 1990. It was part of a 10,000-acre Spanish land grant named Rancho Catacoula that was granted to Colonel Joseph B. Chiles in 1844, and has been a breeding and training facility for thoroughbred racehorses since the 1950s. Jim cut his teeth with one of the trainers of Seabiscuit. He raises and trains the horses while Susan operates the winery. They focus on cabernet sauvignon, zinfandel, and chardonnay.

RustRidge Chardonnay 2003, Chiles Valley— Napa Valley, $30

Historic site and great story. 180 cases produced.

Full-bodied, dry.

Golden delicious apple, pineapple, lemon, and butterscotch notes. Rich, viscous texture with a sweet pineapple finish.

Delicious as a cocktail or with maple-chardonnay glazed shrimp.

Stony Hill

Post Office Box 308
St. Helena, CA 94574
(707) 963-2636
www.stonyhillvineyard.com

In 1943, Fred and Eleanor McCrea bought a 160-acre goat ranch on the northeast slope of Spring Mountain and began planting vineyards in 1947. Theirs was the first winery built in the Napa Valley (in 1952) after prohibition. Assisted by long-time winemaker Mike Chelini and the Roque, Salomon, and Rodriquez families who for generations have worked in the vineyard, the McCrea family continues to focus on dry, steely chardonnay, semillon, white riesling, and gewürztraminer.

Stony Hill Chardonnay 2003, Napa Valley, $27

Unique style.

Medium-bodied, dry.

Mineral, butter, vanilla, and chalky notes. Austere with a silky middle and a long, buttery finish. Delicious with Bay Scallops in Puff Pastry with Lobster Cream Sauce.

The Vineyard at Strawberry Ridge

23 Strawberry Ridge Road
Warren, CT 06754
(860) 868-0730
www.strawberryridge.com

Proprietors Susan and Robert Summer were inspired by their trips
to the Chianti region of Tuscany in the 1980s to open their own
vineyard on 22 acres of hilly Connecticut countryside in 1992. Their
full production of cabernet and chardonnay, from vines over 10 years
old, is harvested and crafted by hand.

Strawberry Ridge Chardonnay Ascot Reserve 2003, Western Connecticut Highlands, Connecticut, $26

Unique style.

Light-bodied, dry.

Aromas of citrus and ripe green apple. Light and creamy, with apple,
apricot, lemon, and sugar cookie notes. Enjoy with grilled shrimp
lightly seasoned with lemon and drawn butter.

Whitford Cellars

4047 East Third Avenue
Napa, CA 94558
(707) 942-0840
www.whitfordcellars.com

Owners Dunc and Pat Haynes along with winemaker Ken Bernards produce small lots of chardonnay, pinot noir, and syrah from their Haynes Vineyard property.

Whitford Chardonnay Haynes Vineyard 2003, Napa Valley, $22

Good value.

Full-bodied, dry.

Pineapple, lemon-lime, chalk, nilla wafer, and butterscotch notes. Vibrant fruit, juicy acidity, a soft, silky center, and well-integrated oak tannins for structure. Enjoy with a silky lobster bisque.

Arger-Martucci Vineyards

1455 Inglewood Avenue
St. Helena, CA 94574
(707) 963-4334
www.arger-martucci.com

In 1998, Rich and Carol Martucci and Julie and Kosta Arger partnered to produce small, handcrafted lots of red, white, and dessert wines. Rich and Carol's son Vincent is winemaker. Kosta and Julie's daughter Katarena oversees sales and marketing as well as hospitality.

Arger-Martucci Saignee Sauvage Rosé 2005, Carneros—Napa Valley, $20

A muscular rosé of cabernet sauvignon.

Full-bodied, dry.

Smooth and creamy with watermelon, sorrel, rhubarb, and cinnamon notes. Delicious with fried calamari or fritto misto with garlic aioli.

Coral Mustang

Post Office Box 1039
Healdsburg, CA 95448
(707) 894-0145
www.coralmustang.com

Proprietors Penelope Gadd-Coster and Frank Coster produce tempranillo exclusively, the noble grape of Spain. Penelope, who worked with notable winemaker André Tchelistcheff, crafts both a red and rosé version from grapes grown in the Vista Creek Vineyards owned by Charlie and Patti Youngclaus.

Coral Mustang Tempranillo Rosé Vista Creek Vineyards 2005, Paso Robles, $21

The best rosé of tempranillo in the U.S. 250 cases produced.

Medium-bodied, dry.

Honeydew, watermelon, strawberry, lemon, and spice notes. Luscious, ripe, and tangy with a counterpoint of brisk acidity. Tangy. Delicious with grilled salmon, ham, or chili cheese nachos.

SoloRosa Wines

Post Office Box 561
9060 Graton Road
Graton, CA 95444
(707) 823-7465
www.solorosawines.com

Jeff Morgan, fellow CIA instructor of the author, Catherine Fallis, and his partner Daniel Moore, looked to the sophisticated dry rosés of Southern France as an alternative to America's favorite pink wine — the slightly sweet, fruity white zinfandel.

SoloRosa Rosé 2005, California $15

A unique combination of Napa Valley sangiovese and Lodi merlot.

Medium-bodied, dry.

Inviting notes of cherry, raspberry, peach, and rose petal combine with a tangy, lemony, brisk palate that is rounded out and given a bit of heft from a few months of barrel aging. The winemakers invite you to enjoy this wine "on the rocks with a burger," but it cleans up nicely and holds its own with the raised pinky crowd.

Syncline Wine Cellars

Post Office Box 761
Bingen, WA 98605
(509) 365-4361
www.synclinewine.com

Syncline founder and winemaker James Mantone began his career at Secret House Vineyards in 1995. Today, he and his wife Poppie make less than 3000 cases annually of select Rhone varietals under the supervision of their two-year-old daughter, Ava.

Syncline Rosé (40% grenache, 28% mourvedre, 20% cinsault, 12% syrah) 2005, Columbia Valley, Washington, $14

Beautifully balanced and full of character.

Medium-bodied, dry.

Peach, strawberry, watermelon, and spice notes. Well balanced with a backbone of acids and a touch of toasty oak. Delicious with seafood or lightly spicy foods such as tortilla chips and fresh mango salsa.

Viña Castellano Estate Vineyard & Winery

4590 Bell Road
Auburn, CA 95602
(530) 889-Bull
www.vinacastellano.com

The Mendez family broke ground on their Auburn vineyard in 1999 and released their first wines, a syrah, a tempranillo, a cabernet franc, and a syrah rosé in June of 2006. They have also planted mourvedre and grenache. Winemaker Chris Markell spent 13 years at Piper-Sonoma, four years as head winemaker at Clos Du Val in Napa Valley, and most recently was CEO of Taltarni and Clover Hill Vineyards and Winery in Australia.

Viña Castellano Syrah Rosé 2004, Sierra Foothills, $16

Brilliant interplay of bold, ripe fruit, and zesty acidity. Excellent for a first release.

Full-bodied, dry.

Strawberry patch, peach, watermelon, and lemon zest notes. Very fruity and full with zesty acid for balance. Enjoy with fish, pork, or vegetarian kebobs.

Westbrook Wine Farm

49610 House Ranch Road
O'Neal's, CA 93645
(559) 868-3499
www.westbrookwinefarm.com

Located near the southern entrance of Yosemite National Park in Madera County, this vineyard and "winery" center around a humble wooden shack belonging to Ray and Tammy Krause. They practice sustainable farming and minimalist winemaking.

Westbrook Wine Farm Rosato Romantico nv, Madera County, $15

One of the driest California rosé's available. 100 cases produced.

Full-bodied, dry.

Made with hand selected bunches of cabernet sauvignon and valdiguie grapes, this is hefty and extremely dry with strawberry, basil, rose petal, and sour cherry notes. Delicious with miso-glazed cod, shrimp scampi, or seitan piccata.

Bodegas Aguirre

8580 Tesla Road
Livermore, CA 94550
(925) 251-9419
www.bodegasaguirre.com

Dr. Ricardo Aguirre, winemaker and manager, Sylvia Aguirre produce nine red wines from 32 acres of land purchased in 1989. He planted 12 acres of grapes in 1995 and made his first commercial wine in 2002.

Bodegas Aguirre Estate Trio 2002, Livermore Valley, $18

Unique style.

Medium-bodied, dry.

This blend of 40% cabernet sauvignon, 40% merlot, and 20% petite sirah is silky, round, and creamy with plum, cassis, green peppercorn, raspberry, vanilla and port-like notes, old-vine richness, and underlying acidity for balance. Delicious with roasted chicken or pork with green peppercorn mustard sauce.

Bokisch Ranches

18721 Cherry Road
Lodi, CA 95240
(209) 334-4338
www.bokischranches.com

This tiny artisanal winery specializes in Spanish varietal wines. Owners Markus and Liz Bokisch lived and worked in Spain before discovering this ranch in Lodi. They farm sustainably, harness solar energy to power the wells, shop and house, and are phasing in renewable biodiesel to replace petroleum-based diesel.

Bokisch Graciano 2003, Lodi, $26

The only graciano produced in the USA.

Medium-bodied, dry.

Dark bitter cherry, black licorice, and dusty notes. Fruit tannins give chewiness; oak tannins are very subtle. Delicious with cured meats, hard Spanish cheeses, Andalusian vegetatble pot, or Asturian bean stew.

Bray Vineyards

10590 Shenandoah Road
Post Office Box 87
Plymouth, CA 95669
(925) 228-2550
www.brayvineyards.com

Bray Vineyards was established in 1996. Less than half of the 50 acres are planted to vineyards from which barbera, cabernet sauvignon, sangiovese, tempranillo, zinfandel, black muscat, and alicante bouschet are produced.

Bray Vineyards Alicante Bouschet 2004, Shenandoah Valley of California, $16

One of only three grapes in the world with red skin as well as red flesh. 150 cases produced.

Medium-bodied, dry.

Strawberry, bramble berry, grape, mineral, tar, and chalk notes. Soft and grapey with chewy fruit tannins as a counterpoint. Polished and very dry. Enjoy with slow-cooked beef with juniper berries.

Casa Nuestra

3451 Silverado Trail North
St. Helena, CA 94574
(866) 844-WINE
www.casanuestra.com

Established in 1979, Casa Nuestra, or "Our House," produces about 1500 cases per year of cabernet sauvignon, cabernet franc, merlot, chenin blanc, riesling, and blends. Owner Gene Kirkham took over the property from his mother in 1974 and began learning about the pre-existing vines. He was joined by current chief winemaker Allen Price in the initial 1979 release.

Casa Nuestra Tinto Classico Oakville Estate 2004, Napa Valley, $38

Made from an unusual field blend of at least nine varietals planted side by side in 1943.

Full-bodied, dry.

Rich currant, blackberry, plum, and tar aromas. Spicy and chewy on the palate, with raisin, black cherry, tobacco and oak notes, and a slightly peppery finish. Try it with flank steak spread with almond pesto.

Chiarito Vineyard

2651 Mill Creek Road
Ukiah, CA 95482
(707) 462-7146
www.chiaritovineyard.com

Owner John Chiarito's first release, in May 2005, was his 2003 negro amaro, a grape well known and loved in Puglia, Italy. In August 2005, he released his 2003 nero d'avola, an important grape from Sicily. As the first USA producer, he had to petition the Alcohol and Tobacco Tax and Trade Bureau (TTB) for use of both of these varietal names.

Chiarito Vineyard Negro Amaro 2003, Mendocino, $30

First release for the winery and first negro amaro in the U.S. 220 cases produced.

Full-bodied, dry.

Crushed strawberries, tangerine, rose petal, lilies, licorice, and cedar notes. Ripe, juicy, and chewy. Excellent varietal character and balance. Enjoy with orecchette pasta with guanciale (cured pig cheek) and turnip greens, or with Caciocavallo, Scamorza, or Pecorino cheese.

Chiarito Vineyard Nero d'Avola 2003, Mendocino, $38

First release for the winery and first nero d'avola in the U.S. 44 cases produced.

Medium-bodied, dry.

Strawberry, cherry, cranberry, hay, fresh meadow, wild mountain herbs, and red licorice notes. Clean and juicy with soft, ripe tannins, and vibrant natural acidity. Long finish. Enjoy with chicken marsala, eggplant and caper salad, or red mullet in onion sauce.

Cooper Vineyards

13372 Shannon Hill Road
Louisa, VA 23093
(804) 285-7533
www.coopervineyards.com

Located on 36 acres in Central Virginia, Cooper Vineyards was founded in 1999 by current owners Geoffery Cooper and Jacqueline Hogge. Winemaker Graham Bell has over 20 years' experience and produces handcrafted wine from several varietals and hybrids, including their speciality, the norton.

Cooper Vineyards Norton 2004, Virginia, $16

A good example of norton. Aged in 100% Virginia oak.

Medium-bodied, dry.

Mouthwatering blackberry, mulberry, plum, spice, and tar notes. Rich and smooth on the palate, with a long, slightly smoky finish. Delicious with creamed beef and biscuits.

Eagle Castle Winery

3090 Anderson Road
Paso Robles, CA 93446
(805) 227-1428
www.eaglecastlewinery.com

Owner and winemaker Gary Stemper, former mayor of Paso Robles and the man who helped build many of the area's wineries through his construction company, has been growing grapes since the '80s. He bought his own winery, Eagle Castle, in 1999 and, with the help of his English wife Mary Lou, designed it to look like an old English castle, complete with moat and drawbridge.

Eagle Royal Red (60% syrah, 40% cabernet) 2003, Paso Robles, $19

An excellent blend incorporating the rich flavors of a syrah with the firm structure of a cabernet.

Medium-bodied, dry.

Aromas of cherry, chocolate, and espresso. Firm, yet mellow tannins. Smooth on the palate, with cherry cola, and espresso notes. Pairs well with savory cheeses such as Brie or cheddar, or try it with poached beef tenderloin.

Fox Valley Winery

5600 Route 34
Oswego, IL 60543
(630) 554-0404
www.foxvalleywinery.com

Fox Valley Winery is located in a 120-year-old, double-walled masonry building originally built to store blocks of ice cut from a nearby creek. Owned by Richard Faltz and his family, the winery produces hand-crafted wines almost entirely from Illinois grapes, including those grown in their own Faltz Family Vineyards, which celebrated its fourth harvest this year.

Fox Valley RA Faltz Vintner Reserve 2002, Fox River Valley, Illinois, $32

Unique blend of cabernet franc, the French hybrid chambourcin, and the indigenous cynthiana (also known as norton).

Medium-bodied, dry.

Spice and black cherry notes on the nose, with a slight earthiness, and a touch of oak. Smooth and well balanced on the palate, with notes of black cherries, currants, and black pepper. Excellent with red-wine braised bison and grits, or try it with fried chicken.

Gelfand Vineyards

5530 Dresser Ranch Place
Paso Robles, CA 93446
(805) 239-5808
www.gelfandvineyards.com

Through years of touring boutique wineries around the world, Jan and Len Gelfand dreamed of owning their own. In 2000, they purchased their 25-acre property in the Paso Robles area, where they have since begun to cultivate 10 acres of cabernet sauvignon, zinfandel, syrah, and petite sirah.

Gelfand Cabyrah (80% cabernet sauvignon, 20% syrah) 2004, Paso Robles, $28

An intense, well balanced cabernet sauvignon blend.

Full-bodied, dry.

Boysenberry, blueberry, raspberry, and blackberry jam notes. Opulent, with a thick mouth-feel, supple tannins, mild acids, and a long, spicy finish. Great with meatloaf and mashed potatoes.

Grands Amis

115 North School Street, Suite 5
Lodi, CA 95240
(209) 369-6805
www.grandsamis.com

Jonathan and Cathy Wetmore transitioned from managing vineyards to making wine. In 2002, they started their own winery and hired South African native J.C. van Staden as winemaker. Zinfandel, syrah, petite sirah, barbera, cabernet sauvignon, and port are produced.

Grands Amis Carignane Reserve Graffigna Vineyard 2003, Lodi, $18

Made with vines from 1942. Historically significant. Good value.

Full-bodied, dry.

Mulberry, cranberry, bitter cherry, espresso, saddle, sauvage, cedar, and vanilla notes. Chewy, lively, and boldly flavored. Enjoy with wild boar, spit-roasted lamb, or earthy cheeses.

Kaz Vineyard & Winery

233 Adobe Canyon Road
Post Office Box 1190
Kenwood, CA 95452
(707) 833-2536
www.kazwinery.com

Winemaker and owner Richard Kasmier, a.k.a. Kaz, his wife, Sandi, and their two children, Ryan and Kristen oversee every detail including creating the labels, ads, and website. They farm and produce organic wine and specialize in unique red blends, rare varietals, and ports.

Kaz "Kazorouge" Someone's Vineyard non-vintage, Sonoma County, $16

Good value.

Medium-bodied, dry.

Blueberry, cherry, orange zest, mocha, espresso, tar, and toast notes. Chewy and slightly tannic with bright cherry fruit and a long, zesty finish. Enjoy with lasagna or moussaka.

Keswick Vineyards

1575 Keswick Winery Drive
Keswick, VA 22947
(434) 244-3341
www.keswickvineyards.com

Located at the 400-acre Edgewood Estate which was part of the 1727 Nicholas Meriwether Crown Grant, Keswick Vineyards is owned by Al and Cindy Schornberg. Michael Shaps, formerly of Jefferson Vineyards, joined the Schornbergs in 2002 as the consulting winemaker.

Keswick Trevillian (touriga, cabernet franc, cabernet sauvignon, and norton) 2002, Monticello, Virginia, $18

Unique.

Full-bodied, dry.

Velvety-smooth on the palate. Cherry, raspberry, oak, and savory spice notes, followed by a long finish. Pairs well with game dishes or paella.

Lenora Winery

632 Main Street
Ramona, CA 92065
(760) 788-1388
www.ramonavintnerscellars.com

Self-taught Swedish winemaker Frank Karlsson learned how to make wine firsthand in his own Ramona Valley vineyards. In 2001, he and his wife Kerstine went commercial with Lenora Winery. They now produce over a dozen varietals from their estate and other vineyards in the Ramona Valley area.

Lenora Dos Rojos (50% merlot, 50% sangiovese) 2004, Ramona Valley — San Diego County, $15

A great blend pairing the smoothness of a merlot with the vibrance of a rich sangiovese.

Full-bodied, dry.

Spicy and earthy on the nose, with notes of black cherry, and allspice. The palate has cherry, black pepper, and clove notes with notes of spice and vanillin on the finish. Delicious with barbecued pork and potato salad.

Winery of the Little Hills

501 South Main Street
St. Charles, MO 63301
(636) 448-2496
www.little-hills.com

David and Tammy Campbell purchased the Little Hills property in 1986, until which time it had served as a tavern. The winery currently produces about 1500 cases per year of native American, French hybrids, and non-*vinifera* wines.

Little Hills Norton Dry Missouri Table Wine, Missouri, $26

RED WINES *Unusual Reds/Blends*

Typical of the fruit-forward style of Missouri norton, which some locals call the "cabernet of the Ozarks." Norton most likely is the oldest native American grape now in wide cultivation.

Medium-bodied, dry.

Aromas of blackberry, plums, and honey. Cherry, dark berry, licorice, and earth notes, with a slightly spicy finish. Goes well with smoked sausage and sautéed onions.

Little Vineyards Family Winery

15188 Sonoma Highway
Glen Ellen, CA 95442
(707) 477-6298
www.littlevineyards.com

In 1996, Joan and Rich Little purchased a 25-acre property from the Hanford Family in Glen Ellen. Joan's brother, Ted Coleman, is winemaker and partner along with his wife Rachel. Their winery was bonded in 2000 and their first two releases were the 2002 zinfandel and the 2002 Resonance, a syrah/cabernet sauvignon blend. Today they also produce the Band Blend—Rich Little plays in a band—as well as a cabernet sauvignon.

Little Vineyards Band Blend multi-vintage, Sonoma Valley, $15

Excellent effort for inaugural release. Unique style. 540 cases produced.

Medium-bodied, dry.

This blend of 43% cabernet sauvignon, 26% zinfandel, 18% syrah, and 13% petite sirah has notes of earth, strawberry, raspberry, mulberry, clove, ginger, and candied orange peel. The dark earthy fruit and toasty oak spice play against each other nicely. Gripping, mouth-watering finish. Enjoy with stir-fried pork or chicken mole.

Niagara Landing Wine Cellars

4434 Van Dusen Road
Lockport (Cambria), NY 14094
(716) 433-8405
www.niagaralanding.com

The land on which Niagara Landing rests has been in the Smith family since 1932. Peter and Nancy Smith, along with Mike and Jackie Connolly and Gary and Lori Hoover, now own and operate the winery. Some of the vines date to the late 1800s.

Niagara Landing Baco Noir 2004, Finger Lakes, New York, $11

Baco noirs often have aggressive acidity. This is an exception to the rule.

Medium-bodied, dry.

Highly aromatic, with aromas of honeysuckle, and strawberry jam. The palate is smooth and fruity, with strawberry, raspberry, and cherry notes and a burst of acidity on the finish. Try it with take-out teriyaki or honey-mustard pretzels.

Spencer Roloson Winery

1207 Randolph Street
Napa, CA 94559
(707) 257-5880
www.punched.net

Winemaker Samuel Spencer and marketer Wendy Roloson founded their winery in 1998, bringing a wealth of wine industry experience together to realize their dream. This young couple has hit a vein with their hip label and incredibly expressive and cutting edge releases. This is the dawning of a new age in California wine.

Spencer Roloson Palaterra 2003, California, $16

One third each of carignane, valdiguie, and syrah. Polished.

Full-bodied, dry.

Game, mint, mocha, tar, wet cement, and dark berry notes. Big, bold, and richly fruity with well-integrated oak and mouth-watering natural acidity for balance. Enjoy with game meats or Epoisses cheese.

Benjamin Silver Wines

1318 East Mason Street
Santa Barbara, CA 93103
(805) 963-3052
www.silverwine.com

Benjamin Silver is one of Santa Barbara's "up-and-coming" young winemakers. In 2000, he founded Benjamin Silver Wines and produces extremely limited quantities of red wine and viognier.

Silver Wine Nebbiolo 2003, Santa Maria Valley, $22

An elegant example of California nebbiolo.

Well structured and earthy, with well balanced spice and fruit notes, and an underlying flavor of leather. Licorice and mild oak on the nose. Drink now. Delicious with linguine in marinara sauce.

WineHaven Winery and Vineyard

9757 292nd Street
Chisago City, MN 55013
(651) 257-1017
www.winehaven.com

Three generations ago, the Peterson family began the cultivation of fields which would culminate in 1995 with the birth of Winehaven Winery and Vineyard. Kevin and Cheri Peterson now operate the winery with the help of their sons, Kyle and Troy.

WineHaven Marechal Foch 2004, Chisago Lakes Region, Minnesota, $11

High-quality example of this early-ripening French hybrid.

Light-bodied, dry.

Bursting with aromas of red fruit and berries. Tart and fruity, with flavors of strawberry, cherry and plum, and a tangy finish. Delicious with salty snacks or a roast pork loin.

Alfred Eames Cellars

11931 4050 Road
Paonia, CO 81428
(970) 527-3269
www.alfredeamescellars.com

Self-proclaimed winemaker, owner, pruner, and vineyard slave, Alfred
Eames developed an interest in wine as a teenager in Spain. His 35
years of winemaking experience culminated in 1995 when he planted
his first vineyard in the high elevations of the Rocky Mountains. He
began selling his wines in 2000. His reds are unfiltered.

Alfred Eames Cellars Pinot Noir 2003, West Elks, Colorado, $14

Excellent value. Purchase by the case!

Light-bodied, dry.

Light tannins and a touch of smoke complement notes of cherries
and dark berries. Smooth and complex, with a rich finish. Try it with
roasted quail or Cornish hen with leeks, black olives, and mushrooms.

Arcadian Winery

Post Office Box 1395
Santa Ynez, CA 93460
(805) 452-7413
www.arcadianwinery.com

Winemaker Joe Davis fell in love with the world of wine while in
college after tasting Domaine Dujac's Clos de la Roche, one of the best
Burgundies (pinot noirs) in the world. In 1985, he started working for
Dan Lee of Morgan Winery and then moved on to Bernardus Winery
where he was general manager. He released Arcadian Winery's first
vintage in 1996.

Arcadian Pinot Noir Sleepy Hollow Vineyard 2002, Santa Lucia Highlands—Monterey County, $45

From a vineyard renowned for its chardonnay and pinot noir.

Medium-bodied, dry.

Ripe cherry and plum aromas with mild earth tones. Round and smooth on the palate, with cherry, licorice, black pepper, and mushroom notes. Enjoy with rare roast beef with glazed carrots.

Arista Winery

7015 Westside Road
Healdsburg, CA 95448
(707) 473-0606
www.aristawinery.com

Al McWilliams, an orthodontist, and his wife Janis, of Texarkana, Texas, along with his brother-in-law, John Copeland and his wife Anne, purchased a 36-acre estate on the benchlands on Westside Road in Healdsburg, in the heart of the Russian River Valley in 2002 and released their first wines in 2003. Pinot noir is the focus, and the couples work with grape growers who farm sustainably while they wait for their vines to mature.

Arista Pinot Noir 2004, Russian River Valley, $28

Russian River Valley at its best is this style of deeply flavored, intoxicatingly perfumed pinor noir.

Medium-bodied, dry.

Wild cherry, Dr. Pepper, sarsaparilla, a mysterious smokey note and an undercurrent of lilac give this silky wine great intrigue. Serve with farfalle (bowtie) pasta with or without chicken in a morel cream sauce, mushroom pizza, or an earthy cows milk cheese.

Arista Pinot Noir Longbow 2004, Russian River Valley, $48

A new benchmark. 220 cases produced.

Full-bodied, dry.

Mulberry, raspberry, cherry cola, wild mountain herbs, mocha, and toasted hazelnut notes. Full, round, and creamy with body and finesse. Enjoy alone or with mushroom bisque or a ripe, earthy cows milk cheese such as Cowgirl Creamery's Red Hawk.

Brooks Wines

2803 Orchard Avenue
McMinnville, OR 97128
(503) 435-1278
www.brookswine.com

Brooks Wines is very much a family affair and a bittersweet story. When founder Jimi Brooks passed away in 2004, ownership of the winery was given to his 10-year-old son, Pascal. Jimi's sister, Janie Brooks Heuck, volunteered to lead the winery, and family and friends have pitching in to carry out Jimi's vision ever since.

Brooks Pinot Noir Runaway Red 2004, Willamette Valley, Oregon, $16

Wonderful example of the varietal at an excellent price.

Light-bodied, dry.

Aromas of red berries and rose petals. Rich and velvety on the palate, with cherry, raspberry, spice, and earth notes. Pairs well with oven-roasted chicken basted in a lemon rosemary sauce.

Brooks Pinot Noir Rastaban 2003, Willamette Valley, Oregon, $50

Benchmark pinot noir for Brooks Wines.

Full-bodied, dry.

Aromas of blueberries, raspberry, spice, and oak. Rich and chewy on the palate, with powerful fruit notes braced by ripe, full tannins. Pairs well with meatloaf or beef Florentine.

Capiaux Cellars

Post Office Box 963
Angwin, CA 94508
(707) 815-3191
www.capiauxcellars.com

Sean Capiaux and his wife Gina founded the winery in 1994. Sean is also winemaker at O'Shaughnessy Vineyards on Howell Mountain. They focus exclusively on small lot vineyard designated pinot noir.

Capiaux Pinot Noir Freestone Hill Vineyard 2004, Russian River Valley, $40

Excellent expression of origin. 153 cases produced.

Medium-bodied, dry.

Earth, tar, smoke, exotic spice, cumin, raspberry, and orange peel notes. Full, round, and silky with soft tannins and a long finish. Delicious with sage-scented veal chops.

Capiaux Pinot Noir Pisoni Vineyard 2004, Santa Lucia Highlands—Monterey County, $50

Excellent expression of origin from the highly sought after Pisoni Vineyard, one of America's top sources of pinot noir. 295 cases produced.

Full-bodied, dry.

Soft perfume and savory notes of roasted quail and red berries. Big, bold, and silky with slightly chewy fruit and oak tannins. Decant for aeration. Enjoy with chicken with porcini mushrooms or Fontina cheese.

Claudia Springs Winery

Post Office Box 348
2160 Guntly Road
Philo, CA 95466
(707) 895-3993
www.claudiasprings.com

Longtime friends Claudia and Bob Klindt and Claudia and Warren Hein
left their lives in San Jose in 1989 and purchased adjoining parcels of
land in bucolic Anderson Valley, Mendocino. Winemaker Bob Klindt
produced 550 cases of chardonnay that year. Since then the Heins
have sold their interest in the winery to the Klindts. Today, the family
produces limited quantities of zinfandel, pinot noir, petite syrah, syrah,
and viognier.

Claudia Springs Pinot Noir Klindt Vineyard 2003, Anderson Valley, $24

1500 cases made.

Medium-bodied, dry.

Cranberry, Bing cherry, clove, and earth notes. Varietally expressive
with a tart, dry finish. Enjoy with char-broiled or barbecued wild salmon.

Clos Saron

Post Office Box 1004
Oregon House, CA 95962-1004
(530) 692-1080
www.clossaron.com

Gideon Beinstock and his wife Saron Rice specialize in pinot noir and
non-traditional red and white blends in a high-altitude location in the
Sierra Foothills. Sustainable farming is practiced.

Clos de Saron Pinot Noir Home Vineyard 2003, California, $45

Benchmark wine. 372 bottles produced.

Full-bodied, dry.

Height of season strawberry, vanilla bean, earth, and "animale" notes.
Very ripe with chewy fruit tannins and supple oak tannins. Long,
earthy finish. Enjoy with barbecued chicken.

Copeland Creek Vineyards

765 Baywood, #147
Petaluma, CA 94954
(707) 765-5997
www.copelandcreekvineyards.com

Philanthropist and environmentalist Peter Pfendlerand (he provides
major habitat building areas for birds and wildlife throughout privately
owned lands in California amongst many other things) is the owner.
Winemaker Don Baumhefner, who cut his teeth with legendary
Joseph Swan in nearby Forestville, opened wine bars in San Francisco
before they were trendy, and then established the wine department
at John Ash and Company, works with Peter to craft terroir-driver
(site-reflective) pinot noirs and chardonnays from their vineyards
on Sonoma Mountain.

Copeland Creek Vineyards Pinot Noir 2003, Sonoma Coast, $30

A bright, piercing expression of varietal and origin.

Medium-bodied, dry.

Strawberry, blueberry, cranberry, peach, tea leaf, mint, and eucalyptus.
Very lively and zesty. Delicious with wild mushroom soufflé, chicken
taquitos, or a ripe Munster cheese.

D'Argenzio Winery

1301 Cleveland Avenue A
Santa Rosa, CA 95401
(707) 280-4658
www.dargenziowine.com

With family winemaking roots in Campania, Italy it was a natural for
the D'Argenzio family to begin to make wine when they settled in

Sonoma. They focus on zinfandel, pinot noir, and cabernet sauvignon from Dry Creek Valley and Russian River Valley.

D'Argenzio Pinot Noir "S Vineyard" 2003, Russian River Valley, $36

Excellent example of Russian River Valley pinot noir.

Full-bodied, dry.

Cherry cola, cranberry, earth, tar, and vanilla bean notes. Soft, round, and silky with a long, flavorful finish. Delicious with roast chicken and wild mushroom risotto.

Davis Family Vineyards

52 Front Street
Healdsburg, CA 95448
(707) 569-0171
www.daviswines.com

Guy Davis, self-titled "founder, farmer, winemaker," started his career in winemaking with Sky Vineyards at the top of the Mayacamas Mountains in the 1980s. In 1995, he produced his first 250 cases of 107-year-old vine zinfandel from the vineyard he purchased in the Russian River Valley and launched his own label in 1997. Today he focuses on pinot noir and syrah as well.

Davis Family Vineyards Pinot Noir 2004, Russian River Valley, $38

Excellent expression of varietal and origin.

Full-bodied, dry.

Brambly fruit with raspberry perfume, earth, and vanilla notes. A big, ripe style with a chewy texture and long finish. Enjoy with "grown-up" macaroni and cheese with aged white cheddar, truffle oil, and freshly cracked black peppercorns.

De Ponte Cellars

17545 Archery Summit Road
Dayton, OR 97114
(503) 864-3698
www.depontecellars.com

Family-owned and -operated, De Ponte Cellars is truly a labor of love
for Scott and Rae Baldwin, who devote themselves to creating quality
wines in the midst of Oregon's Dundee Hills wine country. Thirty-year-
old vines enjoy plenty of room and sunlight, resulting in grapes rich
in taste.

De Ponte Cellars Pinot Noir 2004, Dundee Hills, Oregon, $32

An intense expression of the varietal from 30-year-old vines.

Full-bodied, dry.

Mouth-watering aromas of blackberry, anise, cola, and oak. Robust,
rich, and chewy on the palate. Strong notes of cola and savory spices.
Try it with a salmon fillet and buttered red potatoes.

Domaine Coteau

9150 Three Trees Lane
Amity, Oregon 97101
(503) 697-7319
www.domainecoteau.com

Domaine Coteau wines are produced at the Carlton Winemakers
Studio. It has nine winery operations under one roof. Each is an
independently owned member of the co-op, sharing equipment and
space, and each is separately bonded.

Domaine Coteau Pinot Noir 2004, Yamhill County, Oregon, $28

Unusual expression.

Medium-bodied, dry.

Cedar chest, hay, rhubarb, cranberry, cherry cola, and kirschwasser notes. Very silky and ripe with a long finish. Enjoy with quail with morels, bulgur with dried cherries, or a well-aged Vermont cheddar.

Dutton-Goldfield Winery

825 Gravenstein Highway North, Suite 3
Sebastopol, CA 95472
(707) 823-3887
www.duttongoldfield.com

In 1998, Steve Dutton of the famous Dutton family of grape growers, now in their third generation, partnered with longtime colleague and friend Dan Goldfield to produce the style of refreshing, food friendly wines they would enjoy at home. While their cool-climate Green Valley (a sub-appellation of Russian River Valley) pinot noirs are some of the best in America, they also produce a few hundred cases of zinfandels which are worth seeking out.

Dutton-Goldfield Pinot Noir 2004, Russian River Valley, $35

Once tasted, never forgotten.

Medium-bodied, dry.

Inviting aromas and flavors of cherry, blueberry, sassafras, root beer, anisette, mint, earth, rose petal, and French vanilla and a velvety mouth-feel give immediate gratification, yet judicious oak influence and tingling acidity give it a wide range of pairing options. Serve with eggplant Parmesan, salmon with grilled mushrooms, seared foie gras (while it is still legal), or the nutty Jarlsberg cheese.

East Valley Vineyards

4960 Baseline
Santa Ynez, CA 93460
(805) 455-1412
www.eastvalleywines.com

Situated on a golden, sunny stretch of the Santa Ynez Valley, East Valley Vineyards demonstrates the Central Coast's ability to produce high quality wines. The property was purchased in 1974 by current owner and winemaker David Dascomb, whose grapes have been used by Babcock, Beckman, and Longoria.

RED WINES *Pinot Noir*

RED WINES *Pinot Noir*

RED WINES *Pinot Noir*

East Valley Pinot Noir 2004, Santa Barbara County, $36

Vibrant and appealing.

Light-bodied, dry.

Aromas of plum, strawberry jam, and spices. Cherry and strawberry jam notes, with a tart finish. Try it with creamy mushroom or pumpkin soup.

Elk Prairie Vineyard

11544 Dyerville Loop Road
Myers Flat, CA 95554
(707) 943-3498
www.elkprairievineyard.com

Alan Estrada, a Luiseno and a member of the San Luis Rey tribe, and his wife Sandra established this 10-acre vineyard and winery in 1992 on steep hillsides along Fruitland Ridge. Alan's ancestors tended the vines at California's San Luis Rey Mission. Pinot noir, cabernet franc, and chardonnay are the focus.

Elk Prairie Vineyard Pinot Noir 2003, Humbolt County, $22

Good value. Perhaps the only pinot noir in the world from a Native-American owned winery and vineyard.

Medium-bodied, dry.

Black cherry, cranberry, tar, smoke, earth, and sweet oak vanillan notes. Rich and slightly robust with a long, earthy finish. Delicious with baked Brie, pomegranate lamb, or squash risotto.

Elkhorn Peak Cellars

Post Office Box 821
Napa, CA 94559
(888) 829-5082
www.elkhornpeakcellars.com

Partners John Kryzanowski, a successful stockbroker in San Francisco, Greg Gahagan, one of California's leading solar energy experts, and grape grower Ken Nerlove founded Elkhorn Peak Cellars in 1991. Their Fagan Creek Vineyard, the oldest in the Jamieson Canyon area of Carneros, is the source of their pinot noir. Kent Rasmussen is winemaker.

Elkhorn Peak Pinot Noir Fagan Creek Vineyard 2002, Napa Valley, $30

Excellent expression of origin.

Medium-bodied, dry.

Barnyard, saddle, blackberry, raspberry, toasty oak candlewax notes. Almost syrah-like. Long, chewy finish. Enjoy with shitake mushroom-based or accented dishes or with a ripe Munster cheese.

George Wine Company

Post Office Box 339
Healdsburg, CA 95448
(707) 495-7783
www.georgewine.com

Propietor George Levkoff left his 14-year career as a United States bond trader in Los Angeles after having an epiphany as a result of tasting a Russian River pinot noir with grilled ahi. He set up shop in Healdsburg and never looked back. This budding winemaker sold out quickly of the few hundred cases he produced in both 2003 and 2004. Watch for future releases.

George Pinot Noir Nuptial Vineyard 2004, Russian River Valley, $80

Up and coming producer if pricey. Only 1307 bottles produced.

Medium-bodied, dry.

Clean and fresh with sweet violet, strawberry, cherry cola, rhubarb and leafy notes, lively acidity, and a subtle toastiness. Delicious with duck ragout, Southern fried chicken with country-style gravy, or braised short ribs.

Halleck Vineyards

3785 Burnside Road
Sebastopol, CA 95472
(707) 738-8383
www.halleckvineyards.com

Ross Halleck and his wife Jennifer still have one foot in their previous careers (Ross is founder of Halleck Design Group) while they launch their own small winery. Their one-acre site, intended to serve as a college fund for their three sons, is turning out to produce phenomenal sauvignon blanc, gewürztraminer, and pinot noir. Winemaker Greg Lafollette, formerly of Flowers, vineyard manager Eric Neal, and vineyard consultant Greg Bjornstad roundout the team.

Halleck Vineyards Pinot Noir Three Sons Cuvee 2004, Russian River Valley, $38

Burgundian elegance. 348 cases produced.

Medium-bodied, dry.

Gorgeous Burgundian perfume with cherry, cranberry, strawberry, smoke, sous bois, and cedar notes. Silky and lacy (ironic as it is named after three boys!) with elegance and balance. Enjoy with salmon and grilled mushrooms, or farfalle pasta with truffle cream and freshly-shaved Pecorino.

Hanzell Vineyards

18596 Lomita Avenue
Sonoma, CA 95476
(707) 996-3860
www.hanzell.com

Hanzell is an icon. In 1948, Ambassador James D. Zellerbach acquired this 200-acre estate in the Mayacamas Mountains. In 1953, six acres was planted to pinot noir (this is America's oldest pinot noir vineyard). Current owner Alexander de Brye and his family continue the tradition of crafting Burgundian style (elegant, understated, and minerally wines) today. Three quarters of the production is chardonnay.

Hanzell Vineyards Pinot Noir 2002, Sonoma Valley, $85

Benchmark wine. 220 cases produced.

Full-bodied, dry.

Subtle and closed with notes of earth, mushroom, wet stone, black tea, tobacco, cherry, and strawberry. Decant overnight or open after a few years in the cellar. Enjoy with roast duck and mushroom tartlets.

Harmonique

Post Office Box 160
Albion, CA 95410
(800) 937-1889
www.harmoniquewine.com

Harmonique is a joint effort between long time Anderson Valley winemaker Bob Klindt, owner with his wife of Claudia Springs Winery, and Bruce Conzelman. They produce pinot noir exclusively, using fruit from 27-year-old vines from one of the western-most vineyards in the Anderson Valley, along with fruit from the seven-year-old Klindt Vineyard.

Harmonique Delicacé Pinot Noir 2003, Anderson Valley, $53

Classic varietal expression. 206 cases produced

Medium-bodied, dry.

Mulberry, cherry, cranberry, cola, and mocha notes. Very soft, plush texture with vibrant, juicy fruit and a long finish. Enjoy with poached chicken on pasta with a sherry/truffle cream sauce, or with beet pesto with lavender, pinot noir, and walnuts.

Hop Kiln Winery

6050 Westside Road
Healdsburg, CA 95448
(707) 433-6491
www.hopkilnwinery.com

Owner Dr. Marty Griffin restored his Russian River Valley property's hop kiln, got it historical landmark status, and established wildlife protection in the surrounding area. Along with winemaker Steve Strobl, he crafts high-end pinot noir, and chardonnay from this 248-acre historic ranch.

HK Generations Pinot Noir 2004, Russian River Valley, $36

Inaugural release.

Full-bodied, dry.

Maple syrup, toasty oak, cherry, blueberry, and vanilla notes. Silky and sweet with underlying tart cranberry quality. Slightly astringent finish. Enjoy with duck sausage, mushroom and Fontina pizza, paninis, or with pulled pork.

hope & grace

Beard Plaza
6540 Washington Street
Yountville, CA 94599
(707) 944-2500
www.hopeandgracewines.com

Owner and winemaker Charles Hendricks named his winery after his two daughters. Since the early 1980s he has worked with Viader, Barnett, Regusci, Paoletti, Bacio Divino, and Stelzner. Today he focuses on pinot noir from Monterey and a Napa Valley cabernet sauvignon, and will release shortly a Napa Valley chardonnay and malbec.

hope & grace Pinot Noir Sleepy Hollow Vineyard 2004, Santa Lucia Highlands—Monterey County, $35

From the coveted A-block of the Sleepy Hollow Vineyard, a source of some of America's best chardonnay and pinot noir.

Medium-bodied, dry.

Sour cherry, cranberry, boysenberry, violet, hay, smoke, and mineral notes. Full flavored with delicate structure, soft tannins, and brisk natural acidity. Enjoy with duck confit or Asian-style broiled chicken breast.

Hunter Wine Cellars

Post Office Box 561
Sebastopol, CA 95473
(707) 829-1941
www.chasseurwines.com

After working with Rombauer, Bonny Doon, and others, Bill Hunter
started making his own wine in Sonoma. So impressed with the 1999
Hunter Wine Cellar releases, Alex Bartholomaus, owner of Billington
Imports, offered to invest in the business and became a minority partner. Bill selected the name "Chasseur," French for "hunter," as the
brand name for his wines.

Chasseur Pinot Noir 2004, Russian River Valley, $35

Very Burgundian in style.

Full-bodied, dry. 610 cases produced.

Expressive, earthy Burgundian perfume with mushroom, jam, lilac,
and toasted oak notes on the palate. Very silky with a long cherry
cola finish. Enjoy with spring lamb with pomegranate-mushroom sauce
or with an earthy ewe's milk cheese.

Jack Creek Cellars

5265 Jack Creek Road
Templeton, CA 93465
(805) 226-8283
www.jackcreekcellars.com

Jack Creek Cellars exemplifies the spirit of a boutique winery.
Dedicated to growing grapes of the highest quality, owners Doug and
Sabrina Kruse focus on producing a small quantity of excellent, artisan
wines each year.

Jack Creek Cellars Pinot Noir Reserve 2004, York Mountain, $42

Rich, powerful version of the varietal.

Full-bodied, dry.

Aromas of blackberries, boysenberries, and vanilla. Dark berry, plum, oak, and tar notes. Try it with Japanese glazed salmon with bok choy and toasted sesame seeds.

John Tyler Wines

4375 Westside Road
Healdsburg, CA 95448
(707) 473-0123
www.johntylerwines.com

Owner John Bacigalupi, whose family has been growing grapes in the Russian River Valley for over 50 years, and winemaker Tyler Heck, grandson of Paul Heck, founder of Korbel Champagne Cellars, focus on high quality pinot noir and also produce small amounts of zinfandel. Sustainable farming is practiced in the vineyard.

John Tyler Pinot Noir Bacigalupi Vineyard 2002, Russian River Valley, $42

Made with fruit from one of America's top vineyard sites.

Full-bodied, dry. 826 cases produced.

Blackberry, raspberry, bacon, porcini and cepe mushroom, tarragon, and toasted oak notes. Big, round, and full with deep fruit expression, zesty acidity, and a savory finish. Chef Anne Vercelli recommends this wine braised pork chop with mushrooms, or with angel hair pasta with porcini mushroom sauce.

Kosta Browne Wines

6905 Southpoint Avenue
Sebastopol, CA 95472
(707) 823-7430
www.kostabrowne.com

Partners Dan Kosta and Michael Browne founded their winery in 1997 after illustrious careers in the restaurant business. Their hands-on, artisanal approach is paying off as their pinot noirs gain national notoriety, mainly through the many fine dining establishments which serve their wine.

Kosta-Browne Pinot Noir 2004, Russian River Valley, $38

A distinct style combining perfume and finesse with lavish oak.

Full-bodied, dry.

Textbook Russian River Valley cherry cola and floral notes and fresh underlying acidity, but very full and creamy on the palate with lavish oaky flavors and sweet barrel tannins. Serve with filet mignon, lamb chops, or a very creamy cow's milk cheese.

Kynsi Winery

2212 Corbett Canyon Road
Arroyo Grande, CA 93420
(805) 541-3083
www.kynsi.com

The year 2004 marked the tenth commercial vintage for owners and winemakers Don and Gwen Othman of Kynsi Winery. Don and Gwen source their grapes from Central Coast vineyards, producing about 2000 cases per year of six different varietals.

Kynsi Pinot Noir 2003, Edna Valley—San Luis Obispo, $28

Well-crafted.

Medium-bodied, dry.

Spicy, rich, and smooth. Aromas of black cherry, currant, and herbs, with blackberry, white pepper, cedar, and vanilla notes. Excellent with herb-marinated, stuffed beef tenderloin, or try it with a simple dish of cheese gnocchi.

Longoria Wines

2935 Grand Avenue, Suite B
Post Office Box 186
Los Olivos, CA 93441
(805) 736-7244
www.longoriawine.com

Winemaker Rick Longoria has been in the wine business since 1976 and has served as winemaker at many Southern California vineyards, including Gainey Vineyard. Since starting up Longoria Wines in 1982, he has produced high quality pinot noir, pinot grigio, chardonnay, merlot, and syrah.

Longoria Pinot Noir Fe Ciega Vineyard 2003, Santa Rita Hills, $42

A well-crafted example of pinot noir from the Santa Rita Hills.

Medium-bodied, dry.

This complex pinot noir has a delicious nose of blackberry, cherry, and oak notes. Fruity, with flavors of cherry cola, raspberry and vanilla, and a hint of tar. Delicious with spinach quiche or a rich mushroom and Swiss cheese omelet.

Manzoni Estate Vineyard

30981 River Road
Soledad, CA 93960
(831) 596-0183
www.manzoniwines.com

The Manzoni Estate Vineyard grew from Joseph Manzoni's dairy business in 1921, and later, crop farming. Originally from Switzerland, he settled in Greenfield, Monterey, in the shadow of the Santa Lucia Highlands. He brought with him family traditions of making wine and grappa. In 1990, the family converted 5½ acres to chardonnay, syrah, and pinot noir.

Manzoni Pinot Noir Family Estate Vineyard 2004, Santa Lucia Highlands, $23

Excellent Value.

Full-bodied, dry.

As pinots from Santa Lucia Highlands tend to be, this is a curvaceous bombshell with zinfandel-like berry fruit, mocha, maple and vanilla notes, and vibrant acidity. Long, chewy finish. Enjoy with bacon-wrapped scallops or an earthy cow's milk cheese such as Cowgirl Creamery's Mt. Tam.

Martin Alfaro

496 Hames Road
Corralitos, CA 95076
(831) 728-5172
www.martinalfaro.com

The partnership of Richard Alfaro, a former artisanal baker, and wine industry veteran Joseph Martin, who worked with Richard Graff, focuses on Burgundian style chardonnay and pinot noir along with merlot, cabernet sauvignon, and zinfandel from their 30 acres of vineyards in the Santa Cruz Mountains.

Martin Alfaro Pinot Noir Garys' Vineyard 2004, Santa Lucia Highlands — Monterey County, $39

Garys' Vineyard is one of the top five sources of pinot noir in the U.S.

Full-bodied, dry.

Wild mountain herbs, chocolate mint, raspberry, cherry, cranberry, and vanilla notes. Full and creamy with rich oak tannins and juicy acidity. Enjoy with beef tenderloin braised in pinot noir.

Michaud Vineyard

Post Office Box 716
Soledad, CA 93960
(650) 529-0973
www.michaudvineyard.com

Co-proprietors Michael Michaud and Carol Hastings Michaud bring years of experience to their joint venture. He worked with nearby Chalone Vineyard for 19 years; she is partner and vice president of a wine distributorship. Michael farms the 28-acre vineyard sustainably. Releases include chardonnay, pinot blanc, marsanne, pinot noir, sangiovese, and syrah.

Michaud Vineyard Pinot Noir 2002, Chalone Appellation—The Pinnacles, Monterey County, $35

Expressive of the appellation. 545 cases produced.

Full-bodied, dry.

Menthol, red licorice, blackberry, cassis, cedar, cigar box, and tar notes. Smooth with sweet berry fruit and a chewy, oaky finish. Enjoy with grilled skirt steak with blue-cheese butter.

Muccigrosso Vineyards

21450 Bear Creek Road
Los Gatos, CA 95033
(408) 354-0821
www.muccigrosso.com

Michael and Lynn Muccigrosso planted their vineyards on their Santa Cruz Mountain property in the 1980s. With Jacob Kauffman as winemaker and CEO David Agretelis, they concentrate on estate-grown pinot noir, zinfandel, and a Super-Tuscan blend of syrah, sangiovese, cabernet sauvignon, and petite sirah.

Muccigrosso Vineyards Pinot Noir 2003, Santa Cruz Mountains, $36.50

Rare Santa Cruz Mountains appellation pinot noir.

Full-bodied, dry.

Earth, tree bark, hay, strawberry, cranberry, and cherry cola notes. Sweet, ripe fruit with underlying herbal notes. Smooth and rich. Enjoy with bacon-wrapped scallops or beef tenderloin (or tempeh) with wild mushroom gravy.

Namasté Vineyards

5600 Van Well Road
Dallas, OR 97338
(503) 623-4150
www.namastevineyards.com

Chris and Sonia Miller founded Namasté Vineyards in 2001 on a 200-acre piece of land in Oregon that seemed to them "heaven on earth." All work in the vineyard is done by hand.

Namasté Pinot Noir Prosperity 2004, Willamette Valley, Oregon, $20

Unique style. Made from 20-year-old vines.

Light-bodied, dry.

Delicate floral and fruit aromas. Raspberry, cherry, currant, and rose petal notes. Slightly tart with a fruity finish. Try it with sweet potato tart with caramelized onions.

Namasté Pinot Noir Abundance Vineyard 2004, Willamette Valley, Oregon, $20

Excellent value—one of Oregon's few pinot noirs at this price point.

Light-bodied, dry.

Aromatic and fruity, with notes of strawberry jam, cherry, and hay. Flavors of espresso, cherry, and oak really open up after a few minutes in the glass or decanter. Try it with a hearty vegetable soup such as potato and black olive soup.

Pey-Marin/Mount Tamalpais Vineyards

Post Office Box 912
San Anselmo, CA 94960
(415) 455-9463
www.marinwines.com

Jonathan and Susan Pey, proprietors, bring a wealth of premium wine
experience in both France and California to the nascent Marin County
wine industry. Mount Tamalpais is part of the Golden Gate National
Recreation Area and is being recognized for cool-climate loving varietals
riesling and pinot noir.

Pey-Marin Vineyards Pinot Noir Trois Filles 2004, Marin County, $36

Beautifully balanced and expressive. Extreme good value.
372 cases produced.

Medium-bodied, dry.

Sweet morello cherry, cranberry, strawberry, forest floor, tar, tea leaf,
and truffle notes. Burgundian silk and finesse with slightly riper fruit.
Delicious with quail with morels, seared ahi topped with foie gras and
pinot noir/mushroom reduction, or mushroom/Fontina pizza.

Presidio Winery

1603 Copenhagen Drive, #1
Solvang, CA 93463
(888) 930-9463
www.presidiowinery.com

Founded by owner and winemaker Douglas Braun in 1991, Presidio
Winery utilizes biodynamic growing methods to bring out the grapes'
most natural and intense flavors possible.

Presidio Estate Pinot Noir 2004, Santa Barbara County, $30

From a cool-climate vineyard west of the Santa Rita Hills.

Medium-bodied, dry.

Aromas of soft red fruits, violets, and toasty oak. Cherry, leather, and spice notes. Delicious with sweet, rich foods such as turkey apple sausage and Boston baked beans.

Privé Vineyard

28155 Northeast Bell Road
Post Office Box 3157
Newberg, OR 97132
(503) 554-0464
www.privevineyard.com

When Mark and Tina Hammond purchased the vineyard in 1995, it had already been producing grapes for 15 years. Tina learned how to make wine firsthand through working with her own grapes, producing their first vintage in 2001. They specialize in pinot noir.

Privé Estate Grown Pinot Noir Le Nord 2004, Yamhill County, Oregon, $42

Light, refreshing, and well-structured.

Light-bodied, dry.

Tart and tangy, with flavors of sour cherry, plum, strawberry, and oak. Very food-friendly. Try it with osso buco or a hearty minestrone soup.

Roessler Cellars

380 First Street West
Sonoma, CA 95476
(707) 933-4440
www.roesslercellars.com

Roger Roessler, 35-year veteran of the hospitality business, his brother Richard, consulting winemaker Wells Guthrie, and winemaker Scott Shapley focus on small-lot vineyard designate pinot noir though they recently released a chardonnay as well. Their first release was 250 cases of Sangiacomo Vineyards pinot noir in 2000.

Roessler Cellars Pinot Noir Sanford & Benedict Vineyard 2004, Santa Rita Hills— Santa Barbara, $46

New benchmark producer of American pinot noir. 430 cases produced.

Full-bodied, dry.

Intoxicatingly perfumed with bramble berry, tangerine, cherry, red licorice, and mushroom notes. Luscious, creamy texture balanced with moderate fruit and oak tannins, and acidity. Chalky finish. Enjoy with fresh Monterey Bay grilled salmon.

Roessler Cellars Pinot Noir Savoy 2003, Anderson Valley—Mendocino, $42

New benchmark producer of American pinot noir. 650 cases produced.

Full-bodied, dry.

Softly perfumed with notes of cranberry, raspberry, blueberry, earth, hay, red licorice, and sandalwood. Firm backbone of acidity and a long, refreshing finish. Enjoy with miso chicken or carne asada steaks with fajitas.

Russian Hill Winery

4525 Slusser Road
Windsor, CA 95492
(707) 575-9428
www.russianhillwinery.com

Edward Gomez, retired from a career in academic medicine, and his wife Ellen Mack, a retired physician in academic medicine, established Russian Hill in 1997. This 21-acre estate in the prime Russian River Valley includes a large home dubbed "Tara" by the locals, now the name of their top wine. Chardonnay and syrah are produced in addition to pinot noir.

Russian Hill Pinot Noir 2002, Russian River Valley, $24

This is the best "undiscovered" winery in Russian River Valley.

Medium-bodied, dry.

Opulently spicy with cherry and raspberry notes, vibrant acidity, and a background note of vanilla bean. Delicious with plank smoked salmon, beef bourguignon, mushroom risotto, or flash seared ahi with ponzu sauce.

Russian Hill Pinot Noir Tara Vineyard 2002, Russian River Valley, $38

Benchmark wine. Good value for super-premium pinot noir.

Medium-bodied, dry.

Cherry, currant, raspberry, Earl Grey tea, earth, smoke, and dark chocolate notes. Very elegant with fine tannins and a long finish. Enjoy with truffle-stuffed quail or chicken or with Sottocenere al Tartufo cheese.

Soléna Cellars

213 South Pine Street
Carlton, OR 97111
(503) 852-0082
www.solenacellars.com

Owners Laurent Montalieu and Danielle Andrus Montalieu established their 80-acre winery in 2000. They purchased it as a wedding gift for each other, named it after their daughter—Soléna is a combination of two names that signify the sun and the moon. Laurent is winemaker. They focus on estate-grown pinot noir as well as pinot gris, cabernet sauvignon, merlot, syrah, and zinfandel.

Soléna Cellars Pinot Noir Domain Danielle Laurent 2003, Willamette Valley, Oregon, $45

Brawny style. 381 cases produced.

Full-bodied, dry.

Cassis, blueberry, tar, smoke and vanilla notes. Broad and round with smoky oak and a long tart finish. Enjoy with braised oxtails.

Sonnet Cellars

Post Office Box 2187
Los Gatos, CA 95031
(408) 353-4520
www.sonnetwinecellars.com

After working with benchmark Santa Cruz Mountains producer David Bruce for 12 years, Tony Craig launched his own pinot noir label, Sonnet. Craig was originally a Shakespearean actor from the English town of Newcastle.

Sonnet Pinot Noir Tondre's Grapefield 2003, Santa Lucia Highlands, $32

This wine highlights the quality of pinot noir from Monterey's Santa Lucia Highlands.

Full-bodied, dry. 98 cases produced.

Raspberry, cranberry, rhubarb, mint, vanilla, earth, and stewed tomato notes with a creamy palate, tingly acidity, and a dusty, mushroomy aftertaste. Delicious with osso bucco, Southern fried chicken with country-style gravy, or with a well-aged Gouda cheese.

Stangeland Winery

8500 Hopewell Road Northwest
Salem, OR 97304
(503) 581-0355
www.stangelandwinery.com

First planted by his family in 1978, Larry Miller's vineyard produces very limited quantities of pinot noir, pinot gris, chardonnay, and gewürztraminer.

Stangeland Pinot Noir Stand Sure Vineyard 2002, Willamette Valley, Oregon, $24

Good value for an Oregon pinot noir.

Medium-bodied, dry.

Rich aromas of black cherry, currant, and vanilla. Velvety-smooth on the palate, with layers of dark berries, molasses, and oak. Try it with a creamy fettuccine alfredo topped with grilled chicken.

Stangeland Estate Reserve Pinot Noir 2000, Willamette Valley, Oregon, $40

Excellent example of a rich, powerful pinot noir.

Full-bodied, dry.

Robust and smoky, with flavors of currant, molasses, oak, and bell pepper, this pinot noir is well balanced with a long finish. Try it with veal scaloppine.

Temptress Wines

2517 Northwest 83rd Place
Portland, OR 97229
(503) 730-9633
www.temptresswines.com

Based in McMinnville, Oregon, Temptress wines produces only two varietals: merlot and pinot noir. Winemaker Laurent Montalieu was brought up in the French winemaking tradition, taking his first steps in a Medoc vineyard owned by his great-grandfather and attending high school in Bordeaux.

Temptress Pinot Noir 2003, Willamette Valley, Oregon, $20

Good value.

Medium-bodied, dry.

Smoky, spicy aromas with undertones of blackberries and currant. Silky-smooth on the palate, with cherry, dark bramble berry, and oak notes. Try it with roast beef or a French dip sandwich.

Vidon Vineyard

17425 Northeast Hillside Drive
Newberg, OR 97132
(503) 538-4092
www.vidonvineyard.com

Owners Don and Vicki Hagge focus exclusively on pinot noir from their 20-acre parcel of land in the Chehalem Mountains, located just outside of Newberg and 25 miles from Portland.

Vidon Vineyard Pinot Noir 2004, Willamette Valley, Oregon, $35

Unique style. 268 cases produced.

Medium-bodied, dry.

Earth, mushroom, raspberry, cherry, tar, and oregano notes. Chewy with a tart cranberry finish. Enjoy with grilled salmon or a mahi mahi burger.

J. Wilkes

342 Oliver Road
Santa Barbara, CA 93109
(805) 899-2845
www.jwilkes.com

Jeff Wilkes spent 18 years in marketing at Bien Nacido Vineyards before he and his wife Kimberly decided to open J. Wilkes in 2001. During that time, he learned the potential of Bien Nacido Vineyards for making high quality pinot noir, and for the first few years he and Kimberly focused on crafting only BNV pinot noir grapes. They have since begun to source grapes from Solomon Hills and Vall-Foss Vineyards, and in 2004 they added pinot blanc.

J. Wilkes Pinot Noir Solomon Hills Vineyards 2004, Santa Maria Valley—Santa Barbara, $38

Exemplary of this outstanding pinot noir appellation, proven 15 years before "Sideways" made it a household word.

Full-bodied, dry.

Slight earthy aromas highlighted by tones of cherry, currant, and vanilla. Subtle, complex, and silky on the palate, with notes of dark fruits, spices, and smoke. Delicious with cinnamon and garlic spiced chicken.

Windy Oaks Estate Vineyards

550 Hazel Dell Road
Corralitos, CA 95076
(831) 786-9463
www.windyoakestate.com

After traveling the world, living in Europe and Australia, proprietors Jim and Judy Schultze settled in the Santa Cruz Mountains and planted their vineyard, with 14 acres to pinot noir and one to chardonnay.

Windy Oaks Estate Pinot Noir Proprietors Reserve 2003, Santa Cruz Mountains, $42

Excellent expression of origin and varietal.

Medium-bodied, dry.

Vibrantly fruity with cranberry, raspberry, incense, vanilla bean, and nutty notes. Slight prickly sensation on the palate. Judy recommends this with COTE DE NUITS Baked Goat's Cheese, Mediterranean Lamb Stew, or Grape Harvest Meat Loaf (see Windy Oaks' website for recipes).

Benessere Winery

1010 Big Tree Road
St. Helena, CA 94574
(707) 963-5853
www.benesserevineyards.com

The Benish's fell in love with Napa Valley 10 years ago and decided to buy a vacation home. Learning it was covered with prime vineyards, they became wine producers. With the help of Italian wine consultants and visionary general manager and winemaker Chris Dearden, they have established themselves as one of the best Cal-Ital producers in the state.

Benessere Phenomenon 2003, Napa Valley, $60

Best California Super-Tuscan style wine. 420 cases.

Full-bodied, dry.

This blend of cabernet sauvignon, sangiovese, merlot, and syrah has cherry, black licorice, plum, earth, earl grey tea, and toasted walnut notes. Rich with moderate tannins that will soften with age or aeration. Delicious with a portobello mushroom burger or steak, or with homemade pappardelle with duck ragout.

Showket-Awni Wines

Post Office Box 350
Oakville, CA 94562
(877) 746-9538
www.showketvineyards.com

With the help of Pina Vineyard Management, Kal and Dorothy Showket restored a prime vineyard in Oakville. They had moved to Napa Valley in 1988 along with their son, Ziyad, with the goal of producing wine. Soon Caymus and Dalla Valle were purchasing their fruit. Today with consulting winemaker Heidi Peterson Barrett they focus on sangiovese and cabernet sauvignon.

Showket Vineyards Asante Sana 2003, Oakville— Napa Valley, $50

Same blend as famous Super-Tuscan wine Tignanello (80% sangiovese/20% cabernet sauvignon). 530 cases produced.

Full-bodied, dry.

Earth, tar, smoke, strawberry, cherry, black currant, and leafy notes. Chewy fruit tannins and well-integrated, supple oak tannins. Enjoy with lamb cacciatore.

Eberle Winery

3810 Highway 46 East
Post Office Box 2459
Paso Robles, CA 93477
(805) 238-9607
www.eberlewinery.com

German for "small boar," Eberle produces hearty, robust wines worthy
of their mascot. Owner Gary Eberle began his career in 1973 in his
family's Estrella Vineyard Winery. He opened Eberle in 1983.

Eberle Barbera 2004, Paso Robles, $20

A very well-crafted version of the varietal and a good value.

Medium-bodied, dry.

Smooth and well balanced, this barbera has a warm, earthy nose with
hints of plum, and berry. Soft tannins and jammy flavors are pleasing
on the palate. Pairs well with cheesy, tomatoe-y lasagna and warm
focaccia bread.

Midlife Crisis Winery

1244 Pine Street, Suite A
Paso Robles, CA 93446
(805) 237-8730
www.midlifecrisiswinery.com

Midlife Crisis Winery is fully owned and operated by Kevin and Jill
Mittan. After years of making wine in their garage in Los Angeles, the
Mittans sold their L.A. home and bought 22 acres of prime vineyard
land in Paso Robles. September 2004 was their first crush.

Midlife Crisis Winery Barbera 2004, Paso Robles, $18

Good value.

Medium-bodied, dry.

Aromas of cherry and spice. Appealing fruity tones with underlying notes of cloves, oak and molasses, and a long finish. Decanting recommended to allow the flavors to open up. Delicious served with chicken dumplings.

Noceto

11011 Shenandoah Road
Plymouth, CA 95669
(209) 245-6556
www.noceto.com

Jim and Suzy Gullet established Noceto (Italian for walnut; the ranch has 80 walnut trees) in 1987 and were pioneers of the Cal-Ital movement, bringing sangiovese and other Italian varietals into prominence in the state. Today, along with winemaker Rusty Folena, they produce eight different sangioveses, barbera, zinfandel, a rosé, and Frivolo, a spritzy moscato bianco.

Vino Noceto Barbera Linsteadt Vineyard 2003, Shenandoah Valley of California, $28

On the short list of America's top barberas.

Full-bodied, dry.

Sweet charred oak, dark cherry, blackberry, red licorice, and vanilla notes. Broad and oaky with a long, fruity finish. Delicious with skirt steak, a grilled porterhouse, or roasted eggplant ravioli.

St. Amant Winery

1 Winemaster Way
Lodi, CA 95240
(209) 367-0646
www.stamantwinery.com

Tim and Barbara Spencer and their son Stuart produce a wide array of bold, delicious, juicy, and honest wines, most of which sell out of their tasting room in a strip mall in Lodi.

St. Amant Winery Barbera 2003, Amador County, $12

Best California version of this Italian varietal.

Full-bodied, dry.

With more sun here than in Piedmont, Italy, barbera's home, the wine is fruitier, softer, rounder, and has less acid. With sultry, deep cherry flavors and soft oak tannins, this wine is delicious with grilled meats, pizza, and roast chicken.

VJB Vineyards & Cellars

9077 Sonoma Highway
Kenwood, CA 95452
(707) 833-2300
www.vjbcellars.com

In 1999, brothers Victor and Henry Belmonte and their parents released their first vintage of VJB wines, and in 2003, opened a tasting room in Kenwood. Estate vineyards are planted to cabernet sauvignon, syrah, sangiovese, montepulciano, and aglianico. They continue to focus on Italian varietals such as barbera from Mendocino.

VJB Barbera 2004, Mendocino County, $32

Somewhat mysterious. Shows its character slowly.

Full-bodied, dry.

Young and closed, but opens with aeration (swishing around in a carafe or big glass) to reveal notes of plum, cherry, licorice, mint, mocha, and dark chocolate. Big and balanced. Delicious with lamb shank, sirloin steak, or with Point Reyes or other young blue cheese.

Altamura Winery and Vineyards

1700 Wooden Valley Road
Napa, CA 94558
(707) 253-2000
www.altamura.com

Frank and Karen Altamura established the only winery in Wooden
Valley in 1985. In addition to their focus on their own-label sangiovese
and cabernet sauvignon, they also sell fruit to Stag's Leap Winery,
Pahlmeyer, and Caymus. Charlie Wagner of Caymus mentored Frank,
who also worked with Randy Dunn.

Altamura Sangiovese 2002, Napa Valley, $35

A very polished, elegant sangiovese.

Full-bodied, dry.

Earth, oak, smoke, cherry, and vanilla notes. Round and seamless
with a long, layered finish. Delicious with porcini fondue or penne
with roasted duck.

Bella Luna Winery

1850 Templeton Road
Templeton, CA 93465
(805) 434-5477
www.bellalunawine.com

Founder Kevin Healey has a 30-year history in the winemaking
business, while his partner, Sherman Smoot, is a former commercial
aviator and self-taught winemaker. They focus on Italian varietals,
particularly sangiovese.

Bella Luna Sangiovese 2004, Paso Robles, $28

One of the best 100% sangioveses made in California.

Medium-bodied, dry.

Aromas of blackberry, raspberry, spice, and oak. Black cherry, mild
earth tones, and sweet oak tannins on the palate. Excellent with a
spinach and mozzarella calzone.

Benessere Winery

1010 Big Tree Road
St. Helena, CA 94574
(707) 963-5853
www.benesserevineyards.com

The Benish's fell in love with Napa Valley 10 years ago and decided
to buy a vacation home. Learning it was covered with prime vineyards,
they became wine producers. With the help of Italian wine consultants
and visionary general manager and winemaker Chris Dearden, they
have established themselves as one of the best Cal-Ital producers in
the state.

Benessere Sangiovese 2003, Napa Valley, $23

Best California version of this Italian varietal.

Full-bodied, dry.

Luscious ripe cherries, vanilla bean, and toasty oak notes are
beautifully integrated with velvety tannins. Delicious as a cocktail
or with meatballs.

Dobler Wines

409 3rd Street
Morse, TX 79062
(806) 733-2673
www.barzwines.com

Bonded in 2003, Dobler Wines is the brainchild of Monty Dixon,
whose days in the wine business began in the 1970s when he used
to make wine from wild grapes for his friends. Today, Monty and his
family strive "to keep an honest wine," using time, and gravity as
their primary winemaking tools.

Dobler Sangiovese Bar Z 2004, Texas High Plains, Texas, $22

Uniquely Texan expression of the varietal. Call it the Lone Star State
meets Tuscany.

Light-bodied, dry.

Aromas of ripe red fruit and smoke. Luscious cherry, strawberry jam, and plum notes, with a tart finish. Delicious with Texas-style barbecued ribs.

East Valley Vineyards

4960 Baseline
Santa Ynez, CA 93460
(805) 455-1412
www.eastvalleywines.com

Situated on a golden, sunny stretch of the Santa Ynez Valley, East Valley Vineyards demonstrates the Central Coast's ability to produce high quality wines. The property was purchased in 1974 by current owner and winemaker David Dascomb, whose grapes have been used by Babcock, Beckman, and Longoria.

East Valley Vineyards Sangiovese 2003, Edna Valley — San Luis Obispo, $29

The vintner's first production of sangiovese. 125 cases produced.

Medium-bodied, dry.

Aromas of dark fruit and oak. Cherry, plum, blackberry, and licorice notes, with soft tannins and a tart finish. Try it with portobello mushroom tortellini in a garlic cream sauce.

Eberle Winery

3810 Highway 46 East
Post Office Box 2459
Paso Robles, CA 93477
(805) 238-9607
www.eberlewinery.com

German for "small boar," Eberle produces hearty, robust wines worthy of their mascot. Owner Gary Eberle began his career in 1973 in his family's Estrella Vineyard Winery. He opened Eberle in 1983.

Eberle Sangiovese 2004, Paso Robles, $18

Shows how this Tuscan varietal is suited for the hot days and cool nights of Paso Robles.

Full-bodied, dry.

Complex and supple. Mildly earthy with rich cherry, blackberry, and cola flavors and a long, spicy finish. Try it with filet mignon or beef stroganoff.

Gargiulo Vineyards

575 Oakville Crossroad
Napa, CA 94458
(707) 944-2770
www.gargiulovineyards.com

Jeff and Valerie Gargiulo purchased their Money Ranch Road vineyard in 1992, and an additional nine acres at 575 Oakville Cross Road in 2000. They practice sustainable farming in both vineyards. Valerie's aunt and uncle are the legendary Bernard and Belle Rhodes of Heitz Martha's Vineyard and their own Bella Oaks fame.

Gargiulo Vineyards "Aprile" Super Oakville Blend 2003, Napa Valley, $30

A very ripe style that still maintains elegance and polish.

Medium-bodied, dry.

Cherry, maple, tea leaf, earth, and maple notes. Very smooth tannins and plush texture. Delicious with lamb cacciatore, cassoulet of white beans, sausage and duck, or crispy tempeh risotto cakes with escarole and Parmigiano.

Michaud Vineyard

Post Office Box 716
Soledad, CA 93960
(650) 529-0973
www.michaudvineyard.com

Co-proprietors Michael Michaud and Carol Hastings Michaud bring years of experience to their joint venture. He worked with nearby Chalone Vineyard for 19 years; she is partner and vice president of a wine distributorship. Michael farms the 28-acre vineyard sustainably. Releases include chardonnay, pinot blanc, marsanne, pinot noir, sangiovese, and syrah.

Michaud Vineyard Sangiovese 2003, Chalone Appellation—The Pinnacles National Monument, Monterey County, $30

Expressive of the appellation. 200 cases produced.

Full-bodied, dry.

Sweet Bing cherry, mineral, and toasty oak notes. Broad and creamy with lavish oak tannins that give a chalky, dry finish. Decant for aeration. Enjoy with braised short ribs.

Moonstone Crossing Winery

1000 Moonstone Cross Road
Trinidad, CA 95570
(707) 677-3832
www.moonstonecrossing.com

Owners Don Bremm and Sharon Hanks moved to Humboldt County in 1978 from upstate New York. While pursuing a Fisheries Biology degree at Humbolt State University, he met a fellow student who went on to work in the wine industry. Intrigued, he tagged along and the rest is history.

Moonstone Crossing Sangiovese Fortuna Vineyards 2002, Oakville—Napa Valley, $22

Good value.

Full-bodied, dry.

Very ripe with cherry, mint, framboise, and toasty oak notes. Excellent as a cocktail or with grilled lamb shanks with garlic.

Noceto

11011 Shenandoah Road
Plymouth, CA 95669
(209) 245-6556
www.noceto.com

Jim and Suzy Gullet established Noceto (Italian for walnut; the ranch has 80 walnut trees) in 1987 and were pioneers of the Cal-Ital movement, bringing sangiovese and other Italian varietals into prominence in the state. Today, along with winemaker Rusty Folena, they produce eight different sangioveses, barbera, zinfandel, a rosé, and Frivolo, a spritzy moscato bianco.

Vino Noceto Sangiovese 2003, Shenandoah Valley of California, $16

Excellent value. Best American sangiovese under $20.

Full-bodied, dry.

Essence of cherry and raspberry with soft, seductive sandalwood notes. Velvety with pure, vivid varietal expression and a long, flavorful finish. Delicious with empanadas, cassoulet, or a wild mushroom mille feuille.

Petroni Vineyards LLC

990 Cavedale Road
Sonoma, CA 95476
(888) 290-9390
www.petronivineyards.com

Originally from the village of Montalcino, home of Italy's reknowned Brunello di Montalcino, Lorenzo Petroni fell in love with this estate on Sonoma's West Mayacamas Mountains. It reminded him of home, so he bought it, had 10,000 olive trees air freighted from Pescia in Tuscany, and planted his vineyards. Both are farmed organically. Marco DiGiulio is winemaker.

Petroni Poggio alla Pietra Estate Bottled 2001, Sonoma Valley, $60

America's benchmark Brunello di Montalcino style wine.
1300 cases produced.

Full-bodied, dry.

This serious, 100% sangiovese grosso (Brunello clone) has smoke, cherry, perfume, and vanilla bean notes. Smooth and supple with firm tannins kicking in on the long, dark cherry, espresso bean finish. Delicious with prawns with foie gras butter, calf's liver with bacon cream sauce, or pan roasted forest mushrooms with olive oil and garlic.

Showket-Awni Wines

Post Office Box 350
Oakville, CA 94562
(877) 746-9538
www.showketvineyards.com

With the help of Pina Vineyard Management, Kal and Dorothy Showket restored a prime vineyard in Oakville. They had moved to Napa Valley in 1988 along with their son, Ziyad, with the goal of producing wine. Soon Caymus and Dalla Valle were purchasing their fruit. Today with consulting winemaker Heidi Peterson Barrett they focus on sangiovese and cabernet sauvignon.

Showket Sangiovese 2002, Oakville—Napa Valley, $30

An elegant style.

Full-bodied, dry. 975 cases produced.

Ripe morello cherry, cranberry, violet, and earthy notes. Very supple and round with Barrett's benchmark soft, ripe tannins. Delicious with braised oxtails, portobello mushroom burger, or eggplant mushroom risotto.

Tularosa Vineyards

23 Coyote Canyon Road
Tularosa, NM 88352
(505) 585-2260
www.tularosavineyards.com

A little research convinced owner David Wickham that the Tularosa
Basin would be ideal for growing *vinifera* grapes. He opened his winery
in 1989 with an initial production of 100 cases. As the winery
grew, David encouraged local farmers to follow his example and plant
wine grapes. Today the winery has an annual production of about
3500 cases.

Tularosa Sangiovese 2004, New Mexico, $12

Good value.

Light-bodied, dry.

Fresh, fruity aromas of cherry, strawberry, and blackberry. Pleasing
earthy flavor along with soft red fruits and eucalyptus. Pair with
cheese enchiladas in a lightly spicy mole sauce.

Coral Mustang

Post Office Box 1039
Healdsburg, CA 95448
(707) 894-0145
www.coralmustang.com

Proprietors Penelope Gadd-Coster and Frank Coster produce tempranillo exclusively, the noble grape of Spain. Penelope, who worked with notable winemaker André Tchelistcheff, crafts both a red and rosé version from grapes grown in the Vista Creek Vineyards owned by Charlie and Patti Youngclaus.

Coral Mustang Tempranillo Vista Creek Vineyards 2004, Paso Robles, $32

A very polished, Rioja reserva-like wine. 400 cases produced.

Medium-bodied, dry.

Ripe, supple, and juicy with mulberry, dark cherry, mocha, earth, and vanilla notes. Sweet oak tannins on finish. Excellent with paella, roasted or grilled lamb and beef, and hard cheeses like Manchego and Asiago.

Spencer Roloson Winery

1207 Randolph Street
Napa, CA 94559
(707) 257-5880
www.punched.net

Winemaker Samuel Spencer and marketer Wendy Roloson founded their winery in 1998, bringing a wealth of wine industry experience together to realize their dream. This young couple has hit a vein with their hip label and incredibly expressive and cutting edge releases. This is the dawning of a new age in California wine.

Spencer Roloson Tempranillo Madder Lake Vineyard 2003, Clear Lake, $32

Full throttle style.

Full-bodied, dry.

Smoke, cherry, blueberry, green apple, mint, violet, and tar notes.
Full, broad, grapey, mouth-filling, and chewy with lively balancing
acids. Enjoy with spit-roasted lamb with rosemary potatoes.

St. Amant Winery

1 Winemaster Way
Lodi, CA 95240
(209) 367-0646
www.stamantwine.com

Tim and Barbara Spencer and their son Stuart produce a wide array of
bold, delicious, juicy, and honest wines, most of which sell out of their
tasting room in a strip mall in Lodi.

St. Amant Winery Tempranillo 2003, Amador County, $18

Excellent value.

Full-bodied, dry.

Sweet, creamy oak and bold, ripe strawberry, and mulberry notes.
Rich but balanced. Enjoy with grilled meats, sausages, or
vegetarian lasagna.

Temecula Hills Winery

47200 De Portola Road
Temecula, CA 92592
(951) 767-3450
www.temeculahillswinery.com

Steve and Valerie Andrews, proprietors of Windy Ridge Cellars,
operate this boutique winery, which produces about 5000 cases
a year of primarily Rhone varietals.

Temecula Hills Winery Tempranillo 2003, Temecula Hills, $28

Unique style.

Medium-bodied, dry.

Aromas of ripe berries and prunes. Slightly earthy with intense dark bramble berry flavors, light oak, and a lingering finish. Try it with char-grilled veal chops or paella.

Viña Castellano Estate Vineyard & Winery

4590 Bell Road
Auburn, CA 95602
(530) 889-Bull
www.vinacastellano.com

The Mendez family broke ground on their Auburn vineyard in 1999 and released their first wines, a syrah, a tempranillo, a cabernet franc, and a syrah rosé in June of 2006. They have also planted mourvedre and grenache. Winemaker Chris Markell spent 13 years at Piper-Sonoma, four years as head winemaker at Clos Du Val in Napa Valley, and most recently was CEO of Taltarni and Clover Hill Vineyards and Winery in Australia.

Viña Castellano Tempranillo 2003, Sierra Foothills, $24

Excellent for a first release.

Full-bodied, dry.

Smooth and voluptuous with cherry, strawberry, red currant, vanilla, earth, licorice, hay, and menthol notes. Ripe fruit tannins and well-integrated oak tannins. Decant for aeration and enjoy with lamb shanks with portobello mushrooms and dried cherry, tempranillo reduction.

Anglim Winery

740 Pine Street
Paso Robles, CA 93446
(805) 227-6813
www.anglimwinery.com

Owned and operated by Steve and Steffanie Anglim, Anglim Winery sources its grapes from Fralich Vineyard and French Camp Vineyard in Paso Robles, and from the Bien Nacido Vineyard in Santa Maria. They produce only 2000 to 3000 cases per year.

Anglim Syrah Best Barrel Blend 2003, Paso Robles, $30

Lush, opulent, and well-structured.

Medium-bodied, dry.

Summery aromas of rose petals and fresh strawberries, and flavors of vanilla and blueberry. Enjoy it with bacon wrapped sea scallops.

Bellview Winery

150 Atlantic Street
Landisville, NJ 08326
(856) 697-7172
www.bellviewwinery.com

Bellview Winery is located on the land that owner Jim Quaerella's grandfather bought after immigrating from Italy in 1914. Quaerella is a self-taught winemaker whose lifelong interest in wine led him to plant 25 of his 130 acres with more than a dozen grape varietals.

Bellview Winery Syrah 2003, Atlantic County, New Jersey, $14

Good value.

Light-bodied, dry.

This juicy syrah is fruit-forward with flavors of strawberry and plum, and has well balanced acids and a refreshing finish. Pair with aged hard cheese or salty snacks.

Carina Cellars

2900 Grand Avenue, Suite A
Post Office Box 644
Los Olivos, CA 93441
(805) 688-2459
www.carinacellars.com

Carina Cellars is the result of a fruitful meeting between attorney and
businessman David Hardee and winemaker Joey Tensley of Tensely
Wine Company in 2002. After combining their efforts, the team
produced their first release of syrah and cabernet sauvignon in 2004.

Carina Cellars Syrah 2003, Santa Barbara County, $22

Good value.

Full-bodied, dry.

Aromas of currant, dried cherries, cassis, and leather. Robust and
chewy on the palate, with dark fruit, black pepper, cocoa, and
mineral notes. Delicious with tender turkey in mushroom sauce.

Clautiere Vineyard

1340 Penman Springs Road
Paso Robles, CA 93446
(805) 237-3789
www.clautiere.com

Owners Claudine Blackwell and Terry Brady, whose combined backgrounds include experience in dining, fashion designing, and welding,
have described the winery they opened in 1999 as "A winery...where
Edward Scissorhands meets the Mad Hatter at the Moulin Rouge."

Clautiere Estate Syrah 2003, Paso Robles, $24

Exemplary of the Paso Robles fruit-forward style syrah.

Medium-bodied, dry.

This fruity, juicy syrah has mouth-watering aromas of plum, dark
berries, black pepper, and oak. Try it with pork tenderloin topped with
goat cheese.

Cooper-Garrod Estate Vineyards

22645 Garrod Road
Saratoga, CA 95070
(408) 867-7116
www.cgv.com

Manager and winemaker George Cooper and vineyard manager Jan Garrod, along with members of both families, own and operate this 28-acre estate. They produce chardonnay, viognier, syrah, cabernet franc, and cabernet sauvignon.

Cooper-Garrod Syrah Finley Vineyard 2001, Santa Cruz Mountains, $24

Rare to find Santa Cruz appellation syrah.

Full-bodied, dry.

Subtle notes of cherry, dark chocolate, cherry, blackberry, vanilla, and pink peppercorns. Richly fruity and oaky. Decant for aeration. Enjoy with braised pork loin.

Walter Dacon Wines

50 Southeast Skookum Inlet Road
Shelton, WA 98584
(360) 426-5913
www.walterdaconwines.com

Walter Dacon Wines was founded and bonded in 2003 by Lloyd and Ann Anderson. Walter Dacon was Lloyd's maternal grandfather. Lloyd, a retired professional forester, is the winemaker. Ann, a cartographer with the State of Washington Department of Archaeology & Historic Preservation, is the tasting room manager. They focus on Rhone and Mediterranean wines.

Walter Dacon Syrah C'est Syrah Belle 2004, Columbia Valley, Washington, $28

Rich style.

Full-bodied, dry.

Aromas of blueberry, cloves, and oak, with floral undertones. Juicy fruit notes are followed by licorice, honey, and red pepper. Delicious with prime rib au jus and oven roasted potatoes.

De Tierra Vineyard

503 Corral de Tierra Road
Salinas, CA 93908
(831) 905-1181
www.detierra.com

Tom and Carol Russell with the help of Italian winemaker Lucio Gomero—who is also the largest radicchio grower in the U.S.—released their first wine, a merlot, in 2001. They also produce chardonnay and syrah.

De Tierra Vineyards Syrah 2003, Monterey, $20

Good value. Excellent example of the potential of Santa Lucia Highlands syrah.

Full-bodied, dry.

Sweet bramble berry, earth, mocha, tar, and smokey notes. Elegant full-flavored palate with a juicy, black-pepper finish. Delicious with sausage and mushroom pasta, steak Diane, or a fruity Spanish cheese such as Mahon drizzled with a green, pungent olive oil.

Fralich Vineyard & Winery

1605 Commerce Way
Paso Robles, CA 93466
(805) 434-1526
www.fralichvineyard.com

Owner and winemaker Harry Fralich bought his 20-acre property outside Templeton in 1980. In 1992, he began planting the Spanish and Portuguese varietals in which he now specializes. He sells about 80% of his grapes and keeps the rest to produce about 1000 cases each year.

Fralich Syrah 2002, Paso Robles, $24

Unusual style. Good value.

Medium-bodied, dry.

Smoky, spicy, and slightly tart, this balanced syrah has a long finish. Pairs well with beef Wellington or baked potatoes with all the trimmings. Decant for aeration.

Isenhower Cellars

3471 Pranger Road
Walla Walla, WA 99362
(509) 526-7896
www.isenhowercellars.com

Proprietors Brett and Denise Isenhower, both former pharmacists from Colorado, founded their winery in 1999. They produce a wide range of limited quantity wines from vineyards throughout Eastern Washington.

Isenhower Horse Heaven Hills River Beauty Syrah 2004, Columbia Valley, Washington, $32

Decadent but still light on its feet.

Full-bodied, dry.

This wine has excellent varietal expression with floral and fruity notes along with the Washington State trademark blueberry, mocha characters. Sweet toasty oak notes, ripe supple tannins, moderate acid, and a long brambly, blackberry, boysenberry finish give this wine pairability with fairly full-flavored foods such as pungent cheeses and game (wild boar, venison).

Kynsi Winery

2212 Corbett Canyon Road
Arroyo Grande, CA 93420
(805) 544-8461
www.kynsi.com

The year 2004 marked the tenth commercial vintage for owners and winemakers Don and Gwen Othman of Kynsi Winery. Don and Gwen source their grapes from Central Coast vineyards, producing about 2000 cases per year of six different varietals.

Kynsi Syrah Edna Ranch Vineyard 2003, Edna Valley—San Luis Obispo, $32

Opulent style.

Full-bodied, dry.

Blackberry jam, oak, and dust notes on the nose. Smooth and well balanced, with currant, white pepper, and vanilla notes. Try it with Korean beef or homemade beef stroganoff.

La Sirena Wine

Post Office Box 441
Calistoga, CA 94515
(707) 942-1105
www.lasirenawine.com

Winemaker and owner Heidi Peterson Barrett of Screaming Eagle fame says "the name "La Sirena" means "the Mermaid" in Spanish and Italian. I chose it because I was looking for something fun and magical (like wine) and because I love to scuba dive as well as make wine."

La Sirena Syrah 2003, Santa Ynez, $45

Intense expression of the varietal with very judicious oak use.

Full-bodied, dry. 225 cases produced.

Blackberry, boysenberry, dark cherry, mission fig, vanilla, and mocha notes. Intense with supple tannins and a long, fruity finish. Delicious with grilled lamb with kalamata olives and rosemary, or vegetarian tamales.

Lobo Loco Wines

10497 Alta Mesa Road
Wilton, CA 95693
(916) 687-4767
www.lobolocowines.com

This small Lodi winery specializes in syrah, cabernet sauvignon, and port. They practice highly sustainable viticulture which is certified under the "Lodi Rules" 2005. (Lodi is a big proponent of sustainable, organic, and biodynamic farming. This certification is the first of its type in America.)

Lobo Loco Syrah 2003, Lodi, $10

A steal. Well under market value. Buy by the case.

Full-bodied, dry.

Luscious notes of blackberry, cassis, banana, incense, and tar. Brash, port-like wild berry palate with vibrant acidity and sweet oak notes. Delicious with pork chops with seasoned butter, or bacon and boursin cheese pizza.

Miller Wine Works

Post Office Box 3148
Napa, CA 94558
(707) 254-9727
www.millerwineworks.com

Gary Miller grew up in rural New York and went on to become a professional chef. He is now proprietor and winemaker of Miller Wine Works, where he and his wife Kim focus on small production grenache, syrah, and pinot noir.

Miller Syrah Brookside Vineyard 2003, Napa Valley, $38

Elegant and balanced. 125 cases produced. Good value.

Full-bodied, dry.

Framboise, crème de cassis, mulberry, and white pepper notes. Silky, round, and seamless with a long finish. Gary recommends pairing this

with roast poussin in natural jus with sautéed butternut squash, melted endive and white corn grits (see website for recipe).

Miller Syrah Sage Canyon Vineyard 2003, Napa Valley, $38

Very fairly priced, especially given its similarity to the great syrah-based Cote Rotie wines of France's Rhone Valley.

Full-bodied, dry.

Berry, earth, tar, pink and yellow rose petals, lilac, and pink peppercorn notes. Deep, rich, and round (at 16.3% it should be!), but with brilliant underlying natural acidity and ripe tannins for balance. Long finish. One of America's finest syrahs. Enjoy with a grilled rib-eye steak topped with Point Reyes Blue cheese.

Montemaggiore

2355 West Dry Creek Road
Healdsburg, CA 95448
(707) 433-9499
www.montemaggiore.com

The Ciolino's moved to this bucolic 55-acre estate in the western hills of Dry Creek Valley, Sonoma in search of the pastoral life of their southern Italian ancestors. Vince and Lise produce red wines and olive oils all from estate-grown fruit, and practice sustainable and biodynamic farming.

Montemaggiore Syrah Paolo's Vineyard 2003, Dry Creek Valley, $32

A textbook expression of ripe syrah.

Full-bodied, dry

Gorgeous varietal notes—floral, bacon, hay, grass, and raspberry, with well-integrated sweet French oak, juicy acidity, and a zesty, flavorful long finish. Delicious on its own but better with roast pork loin, lamb chops, osso buco, or a big, juicy steak.

Nadeau Family Vintners

3860 Peachy Canyon Road
Paso Robles, CA 93446
(805) 239-3574
www.nadeaufamilyvintners.com

Self-proclaimed "mavericks," Robert and Patrice Nadeau of Nadeau
Family Vintners produce about 2500 cases per year of big, flavorful
red wines. The winery, which was established in 1997, is located four
miles east of Paso Robles and holds tastings inside the laboratory.

Nadeau Syrah 2001, Paso Robles, $21

Mature and expressive of the Paso Robles terroir.

Full-bodied, dry.

Rich aromas of dark berries, leather, oak, and dust. Round and
velvety on the palate, with layers of blackberries, pepper, espresso,
and smooth tannins. Delicious with filet mignon or polenta and
vegetable casserole.

Ojai Vineyard

Post Office Box 952
Oak View, CA 93022
(805) 649-1674
www.ojaivineyard.com

Owned by Adam and Helen Tolmach, Ojai Vineyard produces just
over 5000 cases per year of syrah, grenache, mourvedre, pinot noir,
chardonnay, sauvignon blanc, and viognier. Adam has been making
wine since 1983.

Ojai Vineyard Syrah Bien Nacido Vineyard 2002, Santa Barbara County, $37.50

Elegant for a warm climate syrah.

Full-bodied, dry.

Richly fruity and spicy with vanilla and an undercurrent of black
pepper. Pairs well with lamb chops or chicken fried steak.

Pacific Ridge Vineyards

7777 Worth Way
Camarillo, CA 93012
(760) 415-5558
www.pacificridgewinery.com

The Pacific Ridge Estate Vineyard has been in owner Bob Kelly's family for over 20 years. Today he sources some of his grapes from Bien Nacido Vineyard in Santa Barbara County.

Pacific Ridge Vineyards Syrah 2000, Central Coast, $30

Excellent warm-climate syrah. 90 cases produced.

Medium-bodied, dry.

Floral, toasty oak, vanilla, currant, and cherry notes. Delicious alone or with roast chicken in rosemary and olive oil.

Page Cellars

19495 144th Avenue Northeast, Suite B235
Woodinville, WA 98072
(253) 232-9463
www.pagecellars.com

Owned by Rochelle and James Page, Page Cellars produces about 1500 cases a year of cabernet, syrah, and sauvignon blanc. Their grapes are hand-picked from Red Mountain and Yakima Valley vineyards.

Page Cellars Syrah 2003, Columbia Valley, Washington, $38

Lush expression of the varietal.

Full-bodied, dry.

Rich and velvety, with notes of cherry, blackberry and raspberry, and a long, smooth finish. Delicious with amaretto chicken or cheese fondue.

Parsonage Village Vineyard

Post Office Box 25
Carmel Valley, CA 93924
(831) 659-2215
www.parsonagewine.com

Bill and Mary Ellen Parsons established Parsonage Village Vineyard in
1998 with a nine-acre parcel of land in the heart of the Carmel Valley
appellation of Monterey. The whole family pitches in to produce about
1400 cases per year of cabernet sauvignon, malbec, merlot, petit
verdot, and syrah, all grown on the estate.

Parsonage Village Vineyard Syrah Estate 2003, Carmel Valley, $36

Rich, warm climate style. 375 cases produced.

Full-bodied, dry.

Varietally expressive notes of boysenberry, plum, blueberry, mint,
violet, bramble, tar, and game. Mouth-filling with well-integrated oak
and a slightly drying finish. Enjoy with pork chops with pancetta,
syrah reduction.

Pax Wine Cellars

3352-D Coffey Lane
Santa Rosa, CA 95403
(707) 591-0782
www.paxwines.com

As wine buyer for Dean & DeLuca in the Napa Valley, Pax Mahle tasted
thousands of wines. Today this 34-year old produces 15 Rhone-style
wines (mainly syrahs) that after only five years have earned him
status as a "cult" winemaker.

Pax Syrah Alder Springs Vineyard "The Terraces" 2003, Mendocino County, $75

Pricey but very Rhone-esque (France's northern Rhone Valley is home
to the world's finest syrah wines). 230 cases produced.

Full-bodied, dry.

Luscious, succulent and silky with earth, game, ossu bucco, violet, lilac, morello cherry, and smokey notes. A wine of seduction. Enjoy with the one you love, in between bites of porcini fondue, sea bass with a syrah, morel reduction, or truffled popcorn.

Peay Vineyards

1117B South Cloverdale Boulevard, #172
Cloverdale, CA 95425
(415) 531-2756
www.peayvineyards.com

Andy Peay, his brother Nick, and Nick's wife Vanessa Wong fell in love with this 48-acre vineyard in the far reaches of northwestern Sonoma after a long search for the perfect site. Vanessa, Nick's wife, earned her stripes as winemaker at Peter Michael, while Nick worked at Newton. She is winemaker, he is in charge of the vineyards, and Andy, MBA in hand, oversees sales and marketing. They specialize in syrah, pinot noir (William Selyem is a customer), viognier, and have 0.4 acres of roussanne and 0.2 acres of marsanne. Sustainable farming practices are in place.

Peay Vineyards Syrah Estate 2003, Sonoma Coast, $55

Handcrafted to reflect origin and essence of the varietals.
575 cases produced.

Full-bodied, dry.

Red currant, plum, mocha, black and white pepper, meat and mineral smokey notes. Cool-climate balance of expressive fruit plus underlying juicy acidity. Enjoy with steak au poivre or earthy cheeses.

Reininger Winery

5858 West Highway 12
Walla Walla, WA 99362
(509) 522-1994
www.reiningerwinery.com

Since 1997, Reininger Winery has offered red wines crafted from
hand-picked grapes. Chuck and Tracy Reininger partner with Kelly and
Ann Tucker, along with Jay and Cyndi Tucker. Chuck is the primary
winemaker, having been experimenting with wine since age six.

Reininger Syrah 2003, Walla Walla Valley, Washington, $32

Lush style with very light oak use.

Medium-bodied, dry.

Fruity aromas with floral accents of rose petals and violets. Black cherry,
spice, and hazelnut notes, with an underlying structure of smooth
tannins. Enjoy with roasted lamb or a smoked turkey sandwich.

Saint Laurent Winery

4147 Hamlin Road
Malaga, WA 98828
(509) 888-9463
www.saintlaurent.net

Michael and Laura Laurent Mrachek started their career as fruit growers
with a few acres of cherries in 1978. They now farm merlot, syrah,
and cabernet sauvignon on 260 acres in Columbia Valley.

St. Laurent Syrah 2003, Columbia Valley, Washington, $20

Good value.

Full-bodied, dry.

Richly flavored with leather, oak, and molasses. Velvety with medium
oak tannins and a long finish. Excellent with hard cheeses such as
Pecorino Romano or with roast beef.

Sand T Cellars

3194 Redwood Road
Napa, CA 94558
(707) 252-6690
www.sandtcellars.com

Tom and Susan Ridley moved to the Napa Valley 30 years ago to live in the peaceful countryside. Neighbor George Hendry of Hendry Cellars urged them to plant the three-acre meadow in front of their house. They named it Brookside Vineyard since the Redwood Creeks flows through the property. In 2001, Gary Miller purchased syrah from Brookside and the rest was history. It is now a highly sought after source of syrah.

Sand T Cellars Syrah Brookside Vineyard 2004, Napa Valley, $26

Syrah-master Gary Miller "discovered" this vineyard source.
150 cases produced.

Full-bodied, dry.

Very enticing with berry, black and green peppercorn, lilac, and vanilla bean notes. Light oak tannins and a long, chewy finish. Decant for aeration. Enjoy with flank steak with green peppercorn mustard sauce.

Shadow Canyon Cellars

846 Higuera Street, #5
San Luis Obispo, CA 93401
(805) 781-9400
www.shadowcanyon.com

Owner and winemaker Gary Gibson bought his York Mountain property
in 1996 and has been making high quality wines ever since. Both his
syrah and his pinot blanc are widely acclaimed, and his syrah grapes
have been used for Manfred Krankl's famed Sine Qua Non wines.

Shadow Canyon Cellars Syrah 2003, York Mountain—San Luis Obispo, $45

Made by a winemaker to watch.

Full-bodied, dry.

Rich aromas of dark berries, vanilla, cherry cola, and licorice. Currant,
oak, and white pepper notes on the palate, with a long, spicy finish.
Pair it with cream of mushroom soup or a seared fillet with a rich pink
peppercorn sauce.

Soléna Cellars

213 South Pine Street
Carlton, OR 97111
(503) 852-0082
www.solenacellars.com

Owners Laurent Montalieu and Danielle Andrus Montalieu established
their 80-acre winery in 2000. They purchased it as a wedding gift for
each other, named it after their daughter—Soléna is a combination of
two names that signify the sun and the moon. Laurent is winemaker.
They focus on estate-grown pinot noir as well as pinot gris, cabernet
sauvignon, merlot, syrah, and zinfandel.

Soléna Cellars Syrah 2003, Del Rio—Rogue Valley, Oregon, $30

Unique style. 350 cases produced.

Full-bodied, dry.

Boysenberry, cherry, black currant, spicy oak, and cayenne pepper notes. Smooth and well balanced. Enjoy with tender chicken breasts with a mild caponata sauce.

Summerwood Winery

2175 Arbor Road
Paso Robles, CA 93446
(415) 310-0163
www.summerwoodwine.com

After earning a degree in enology from Fresno State University, Summerwood winemaker Scott Hawley studied with winemakers from around the world to develop his craft. He creates rich, intense wines that reflect the unique Paso Robles terroir.

Summerwood Syrah Diosa 2003, Paso Robles, $52

Decadent style.

Full-bodied, dry.

Robust and earthy, with aromas of cassis. Layers of blackberry and toasty oak. Well balanced, with a round, velvety mouth-feel and a long finish. Pair with roast Cornish game hen in a blackberry reduction sauce.

Syncline Wine Cellars

307 West Humboldt Street
Post Office Box 761
Bingen, WA 98605
(509) 365-4361
www.synclinewine.com

Syncline founder and winemaker James Mantone began his career at Secret House Vineyards in 1995. Today, he and his wife Poppie make less than 3000 cases annually of select Rhone varietals under the supervision of their two-year-old daughter Ava.

Syncline Syrah Milbrandt Vineyards 2004, Columbia Valley, Washington, $22

Good value.

Medium-bodied, dry.

Mouth-watering aromas of blackberries, bay leaves, and hay. Flavors of anise, vanilla, and oak and a long, silky finish. Pair with rich French cassoulet.

Tularosa Vineyards

23 Coyote Canyon Road
Tularosa, NM 88352
(505) 585-2260
www.tularosavineyards.com

A little research convinced owner David Wickham that the Tularosa Basin would be ideal for growing *vinifera* grapes. He opened the winery in 1989 with an initial production of 100 cases. As the winery grew, David encouraged local farmers to follow his example and plant grapes. Today the winery has an annual production of about 3500 cases

Tularosa Shiraz Table Wine 2004, New Mexico, $10

A unique expression of the varietal at a moderate price point.

Medium-bodied, dry.

Aromas of cherry, blueberry, and green olive, with a hint of tar. Juicy notes of blackberry, raisin, and black pepper, with a long, spicy finish. Try it with chicken Parmigiano and toasted garlic bread.

Wildwood Vineyard & Winery

555 El Camino Real
San Luis Obispo, CA 93401
(805) 546-1088
www.wildwoodwine.com

Owned and operated by the Wood family, Wildwood Winery is located on 80 acres between Edna Valley and Paso Robles. The first vines were planted in 1999 with the help of Cal Poly viticulture graduates Pete Hoffman and Charles Kidd. Charles is now vineyard manager.

Wildwood Syrah Sheri's Vineyard 2003, Central Coast, $28

Excellent expression of the varietal.

Medium-bodied, dry.

Aromas of blueberry and vanilla. Round and soft on the palate with notes of dark berries, spices, and tar. Try it with grilled chicken breast or vegetable lasagna.

Willis Hall

4715 126th Street Northeast
Marysville, WA 98271
(360) 653-1247
www.willishall.com

Winemaker and owner John Bell, a former employee of the Boeing Company, retired in 2004 to begin making wine full time. A largely self-taught winemaker, his experience comes from years of interest in wine and what he learned as a member of the Boeing Wine Club.

Willis Hall Syrah Chandler Reach Vineyards 2003, Yakima Valley, Washington, $26

Very well balanced.

Medium-bodied, dry.

Rich flavors of cherry and molasses and a hint of black pepper. Smooth texture. Long finish. It pairs well with bold, flavored meats such as herb-marinated steak.

Cass Vineyards and Winery

7350 Linne Road
Paso Robles, CA 93446
(805) 239-1730
www.casswines.com

Opened by Steve Cass in 2005, Cass Vineyards produces 100% estate-grown wines. The winery specializes in Rhone varietals and conducts cooking classes focusing on fare from around the world.

Cass Grenache/Syrah (90%/10%) Blend Rockin' One 2004, Paso Robles, $34

A great example of a Grenache-based blend.

Light-bodied, dry.

Fruity aromas with underlying notes of oak. Tart and tangy on the palate, with cherry, strawberry, and plum notes. Try it with balsamic glazed pork chops.

Marilyn Remark-Burnstein Remark Winery

645 River Road
Salinas, CA 93908
(831) 455-9310
www.remarkwines.com

Marilyn Remark and Joel Burnstein love Rhone grape varietals for their compatibility with the Mediterranean diet. He was a former stock trader. Today they produce roussanne, marsanne, rosé, grenache, petite sirah, and syrah.

Marilyn Remark Grenache Wild Horse Road Vineyard 2003, Monterey County, $45

Easily in the top 10 grenaches of the world.

Full-bodied, dry.

Earth, tar, cherry, strawberry, stewed fruits, and cinnamon notes. Big, full, fruity, and well-structured. Chewy and vibrant. Enjoy with pappardelle noodles with duck ragout or braised lentils with eggplant and mushrooms.

T-Vine Cellars

Post Office Box 1115
Calistoga, CA 94515-6115
(707) 942-8685
www.tvinecellars.com

Owner and winemaker Greg Brown celebrates his fifteenth vintage with the 2003 releases. After majoring in Finance at Chico State, Greg worked as a Bank Vice President for five years. During this time he was an avid collector of wine and befriended many winemakers. One of them invited him to work crush. He gave notice, left the world of finance, and hasn't turned back since.

T-Vine Grenache 2004, Napa Valley, $28

Benchmark wine. 700 cases produced.

Full-bodied, dry.

Intense notes of cherry cola, strawberry jam, and freshly ground black peppercorns. Broad and rich with lively acidity and very soft tannins. Enjoy with spicy Pasta Fra Diavolo with sausage instead of shrimp or lobster, or with Niman Ranch Beef burgers with the works.

Dobler Wines

409 3rd Street
Morse, TX 79062
(806) 733-2673
www.barzwines.com

Bonded in 2003, Dobler Wines is the brainchild of Monty Dixon, whose days in the wine business began in the 1970s when he used to make wine from wild grapes for his friends. Today, Monty and his family strive "to keep an honest wine," using time and gravity as their primary winemaking tools and with limited filtration.

Dobler Wines Mourvedre Bar Z 2004, Texas High Plains, Texas, $22

Excellent example of warm-climate loving mourvedre.

Light-bodied, dry.

Fresh and fruity, with aromas of cherry, vanilla and molasses, and lip-smacking flavors of blackberry, plum, and black pepper. Tasty with a hamburger and fries, or try it with filet mignon and rosemary mashed potatoes

Amphora Winery

4791 Dry Creek Road, Building 6
Healdsburg, CA 95448
(707) 431-7767
www.amphorawines.com

Winemaker and co-owner Rick Hutchinson combines his love of pottery and winemaking at the winery, named after those vessels used to store and transport wine in Greek and Roman times. In 1997, the "winery" was in the basement of a prune barn. In spring, 2006 they relocated to a larger space complete with artist studios to accommodate the growth to current levels of 3500 cases. From the original petite sirah, and zinfandel, Rick has expanded the line to include cabernet sauvignon, merlot, and syrah.

Amphora Mounts Vineyard Petite Sirah 2004, Dry Creek Valley, $32

Hands down, America's finest petite sirah.

Lip-smacking flavors of ripe blackberries and huckleberries and dark chocolate with a dash of freshly ground black pepper. Delicious with barbecued tri-tip, grilled sausages, or sweet, tangy cheddars.

Vincent Arroyo

2361 Greenwood Avenue
Calistoga, CA 94515
(707) 942-6995
www.vincentarroyo.com

The very humble Vincent Arroyo is known as a petite sirah master, and today has such a loyal following for this along with his cabernet sauvignon and cabernet sauvignon/syrah/petite sirah blend, "Entrada," that he sells only consumer direct to his loyal customer base.

Vincent Arroyo Petite Sirah 2004, Napa Valley, $32

Good value. 1000 cases produced.

Full-bodied, dry.

Herbs de Provence, pink peppercorn, blackberry, huckleberry, and boysenberry notes. Chewy and vibrantly flavored. Very long finish. Enjoy with St. Louis style ribs.

Gelfand Vineyards

5530 Dresser Ranch Place
Paso Robles, CA 93446
(805) 239-5808
www.gelfandvineyards.com

Through years of touring small, family-owned wineries around the world, Jan and Len Gelfand dreamed of owning their own. In 2000, they purchased their 25-acre property in the Paso Robles area, where they have since begun to cultivate 10 acres of cabernet sauvignon, zinfandel, syrah, and petite sirah.

Gelfand Petite Sirah 2004, Paso Robles, $30

Good candidate for aging. Full-bodied, dry.

Rich with cherry, boysenberry, and spice notes. Velvety mouth-feel with bracing acids and with a long, rich finish. Pairs well with prime rib and scalloped potatoes.

Victor Hugo Vineyards

2850 El Pomar Drive
Templeton, CA 93465
(805) 434-1128
www.victorhugowinery.com

Owner and winemaker Victor Hugo Roberts started his career in the wine industry in 1982 after getting his degree in enology from U.C. Davis. He and his wife Leslie planted their first grapes in 1985 and soon began to make wines in a 100-year-old barn on their land in Templeton.

Victor Hugo Petite Sirah 2003, Paso Robles, $18

Excellent petite sirah from 20-year-old vines.

Medium-bodied, dry.

Raspberry, cherry, and slight earthy aromas. Smooth and round on the palate, with flavors of cherry cola, almonds and vanilla, and a lingering finish. Try it with roasted turkey with pecan stuffing.

Mettler Family Vineyards

Post Office Box 403
Victor, CA 95253
(888) 509-5969
www.mettlerwine.com

With 100-year-old vineyard properties and eight generations of wine industry experience, the Mettler family is a force in Lodi. They were one of the first families to introduce French clones here. Organic and biologically integrated farming systems are in place to insure the highest quality fruit.

Mettler Family Vineyards Petite Sirah 2003, Lodi, $22

Full throttle warm climate style without heavy oak influence.

Full-bodied, dry.

Menthol, mission fig, mocha, blackberry, and floral notes. Very round, mouth-coating, and supple. Extremely well balanced with added complexity from healthy old vines. Delicious with Morrocan-spiced lamb chops, kasha with spicy maple pecans, or Gouda cheese.

Shannon Ridge

Post Office Box 2037
Clearlake Oaks, CA 95423
(707) 998-9656
www.shannonridge.com

Owners Clay and Margarita Shannon met while working at the same Napa winery. In 1995, they visited a property perched atop a steep mountain ridge about 35 miles north of the Napa county line. Cooled by winds off of nearby Clear Lake, and with lean, volcanic soils, the couple knew they were home. Vineyard Manager Celestino Castañeda and winemaker Marco DiGiulio oversee the growing and production of zinfandel, cabernet sauvignon, barbera, petite sirah, and sauvignon blanc from this rugged site.

Shannon Ridge Petite Sirah 2002, Lake County, $27

Textbook varietal expression. Good value.

Full-bodied, dry.

Lusciously fruity with blueberry, boysenberry, mulberry, Asian five-spice, tar, and forest floor notes. Vibrant, expressive, and unadulterated with balancing juicy acidity and a judicious use of oak. Enjoy with grilled London Broil.

Six Hands Winery

13783 Isleton Road
Post Office Box 444
Walnut Grove, CA 95690
(916) 776-2053
www.sixhandswinery.com

Owner Peter Marks has a wine heritage going back several generations. His great-grandfather, Joseph Machado, farmed the land here and his grandfather Bill Guerard taught him the art of winemaking. With his degree from U.C. Davis in Plant Sciences and Enology, and his wife Richele's expertise in genetics, the couple realized the natural potential of the Delta and set up their winery on the family's century-old ranch.

Six Hands Petite Sirah Heringer Holland Vineyard 2003, Clarksburg, $13

Good value.

Medium-bodied, dry.

Cherry, menthol, and delicate raspberry notes. Lightly fruity with juicy acidity. Enjoy with sausage and mushroom pizza, ribs, or with grilled vegetables.

T-Vine Cellars

Post Office Box 1115
Calistoga, CA 94515-6115
(707) 942-8685
www.tvinecellars.com

Owner and winemaker Greg Brown celebrates his fifteenth vintage
with the 2003 releases. After majoring in Finance at Chico State, Greg
worked as a Bank Vice President for five years. During this time he
was an avid collector of wine and befriended many winemakers. One
of them invited him to work crush. He gave notice, left the world of
finance, and hasn't turned back since.

T-Vine Petite Sirah Frediani Vineyard 2003, Napa Valley, $34

Big-boned but balanced. 720 cases produced.

Full-bodied, dry.

Young and closed, but opens with aeration. Dark berry, violet,
rosemary, clove, bacon, and menthol notes. Decadent style with juicy,
accessible fruit, and well-integrated oak. Delicious with sirloin steak,
or with Catalan-style lima bean stew with sausages and mint.

Allora Vineyards

Post Office Box 1008
St. Helena, CA 94574
(707) 963-1227
www.alloravineyards.com

Terry and Nancy Klein established Allora Vineyards in 1999, retiring
from their very successful plastering business to concentrate on making
small production, high quality wine. Consulting winemaker Rudy
Zuidema of Robert Craig Wine Cellars and Wirra Wirra Winery in
Australia continues to work primarily with cabernet sauvignon.

Allora Vineyards Cielo Red Proprietary Blend 2003, Napa Valley, $30

Good value. 200 cases produced.

Full-bodied, dry.

This blend of cabernet sauvignon, cabernet franc, and merlot has
tobacco, tar, cherry, and bark notes. Rich, soft, and mouth-coating with
a chewy, slightly tart finish. Enjoy with braised lamb shanks, rib-eye
steak, or aged dry Jack or Camembert cheese.

Bedell North Fork LLC

36225 Main Road (Route 25)
Cutchogue, NY 11935
(631) 765-4168
www.bedellcellars.com

Owner Michael Lynne, Co-Chairman and Co-CEO of New Line Cinema,
met founding winemaker Kip Bedell who had established the seven-
acre Bedell Vineyards at the site of an old potato farm. He now
oversees the 78-acre property along with winemaker John Irving
Levenberg. Vineyard Manager Dave Thompson is a member of the
board of the Long Island Sustainable Agriculture program.

Bedell Cellars Cupola 2001, North Fork of Long Island, New York, $30

Understated and elegant Bordeaux style wine.

Medium-bodied, dry.

This blend of 51% cabernet sauvignon, 22% cabernet franc, 22% merlot, and 5% petit verdot has notes of cassis, dark cherry, black peppercorns, tarragon, mint, and curried lamb. Very appealing texture with a dry, gripping finish. Enjoy with rack of lamb or Affineur Jean d'Alos, an earthy cheese from Bordeaux.

Chateau Faire Le Pont

389 Technology Center Way
Wenatchee, WA 98801
(509) 670-0422
www.fairelepont.com

Located in a renovated 1920s brick warehouse, Chateau Faire Le Pont produces 3000 cases a year from Yakima Valley, Alderdale, and Mattawa grapes. Doug and Debé Brazil founded the winery in 2004, fulfilling a lifelong dream of Doug, a former Navy helicopter pilot. They encourage wine lovers to learn about wine firsthand through their "adopt-a-vine program."

Chateau Faire le Pont Bordeaux Blend Confluence (cabernet sauvignon, merlot, cabernet franc) 2003, Yakima Valley, Washington, $39

One of Washington's better Bordeaux blends.

Medium-bodied, dry.

Satiny smooth on the palate, with rich notes of cherry, blackberry, spice, oak, and vanilla. Complex and elegant. Great with pan seared chicken breasts with olives and mushrooms.

Ciccone Vineyard & Winery

10343 East Hilltop Road
Suttons Bay, MI 49682
(231) 271-5553
www.cicconevineyards.com

Owned and operated by Silvio Tony Ciccone—also known as the father of Madonna—and his wife Joan, Ciccone Vineyards is one of a growing number of wineries in Michigan's relatively temperate Leelanau Peninsula. They produce about 2200 cases per year of over a dozen varietals, all harvested and crafted by hand.

Ciccone Red Blend Lee La Tage (cabernet sauvignon, cabernet franc, merlot, and malbec) 2004, Leelanau Peninsula, Michigan, $16

Unique style.

Medium-bodied, dry.

Aromas of cinnamon and ripe berries. Round and smooth on the palate, with cherry, white pepper, allspice, and black olive notes. Excellent balance of acids and tannins. Great with lentil soup or steak carpaccio.

Nicholas Cole Cellars

705 Berney Drive
Walla Walla, WA 99362
(509) 525-0608
www.nicholascolecellars.com

Mike Neuffer's dream of owning his own winery took shape in the 1980s as he began to learn about and collect fine wines. In 1999, he began touring the great winegrowing regions of California and Washington, and in 2001, he founded Nicholas Cole Cellars. He was joined by winemaker Chris Camarda of Andrew Will Winery.

Nicholas Cole Camille (merlot, cabernet sauvignon, and cabernet franc) Bordeaux Blend 2003, Columbia Valley, Washington, $48

Dense, bold style.

Full-bodied, dry.

Aromas of cherries, raspberries, and a slight earthiness. Lush and velvety on the palate, with blackberry, boysenberry, earth, black pepper, and tar notes. Delicious with rack of lamb or washed-rind cheeses such as Epoisses or Taleggio.

Lail Vineyards

320 Stoneridge Road
Angwin, CA 94508
(707) 968-9900
www.lailvineyards.com

Owner Robin Lail's great granduncle, Gustav Niebaum, founded
Inglenook Vineyards in 1879. Today with internationally reknowned
winemaker Philippe Melka, she crafts pure, complete, and expressive
wines that are built for the long haul.

Lail Vineyards J. Daniel Cuvee 2002, Napa Valley, $75

Benchmark wine not only for a Bordeaux blend but also for the USA.

Full-bodied, dry.

This cabernet sauvignon-dominated blend is one of the best American
wines, period. Full, lusciously fruited, and complex with plum, cassis,
black cherry, smoke, and tobacco notes. Eminently drinkable now, but
very ageable. Delicious with noisettes of lamb, beef Wellington, or thin
crust pizza topped with well-aged Gouda, aged balsamic vinegar, and
porcini dust.

O'Brien Family Vineyard

Post Office Box 6020
Napa, CA 94558
(707) 252-8463
www.obrienfamilyvineyard.com

In March 2000, Bart and Barb O'Brien purchased the former Costello
Winery in the Oak Knoll District of Napa Valley. With the help of vine-
yard and cellar manager Michael Hanna, the great-great-grandson of
John Muir, winemaker Dave Cofran formerly of Silver Oak Cellars, and
consulting winemaker Hugh Chappelle (Flowers Vineyards and now
Lynmar), they produce chardonnay, merlot, and a Bordeaux blend.

O'Brien Family Vineyard Seduction 2003, Napa Valley, $28

A Bordeaux blend, but tastes more like a Tuscan blend.

Full-bodied, dry.

This blend of cabernet sauvignon, merlot, and cabernet franc has dark bitter cherry, boysenberry, mulberry, menthol, rosemary, and vanilla notes. Round and voluptuous with juicy natural acids and sweet oak tones. Long finish. Enjoy with Florentine pork roast.

Page Cellars

19495 144th Avenue Northeast, Suite B235
Woodinville, WA 98072
(253) 232-9463
www.pagecellars.com

Owned by Rochelle and James Page, Page Cellars produces about 1500 cases a year of cabernet, syrah, and sauvignon blanc. Their grapes are hand-picked from Red Mountain and Yakima Valley vineyards.

Page Cellars Bordeaux Blend Preface (84% cabernet sauvignon, 16% cabernet franc) 2003, Red Mountain, Washington, $38

Big, bold, and beautifully balanced.

Full-bodied, dry.

Aromas of cedar, cherry, and plum. Well balanced and smooth on the palate, with black cherry, and currant notes. Delicious with portobello mushroom and goat cheese pizza, or with cranberry and pecan-stuffed sirloin roast.

Parsonage Village Vineyard

Post Office Box 25
Carmel Valley, CA 93924
(831) 659-2215
www.parsonagewine.com

Bill and Mary Ellen Parsons established Parsonage Village Vineyard in 1998 with a nine-acre parcel of land in the heart of the Carmel Valley appellation of Monterey. The whole family pitches in to produce about 1400 cases per year of cabernet sauvignon, malbec, merlot, petit verdot, and syrah, all grown on the estate.

Parsonage Village Vineyard Petite Appliqué Reserve Red 2003, Carmel Valley, $75

Very rare petit verdot-dominated blend. 50 cases produced.

Full-bodied, dry.

Very tangy and savory with cranberry, Bing cherry, shaved almond, seashell, chalk, and cured meats notes. Very structured and taut with chewy fruit tannins and juicy natural acidity. Enjoy with guanciale (pig cheeks) risotto.

Portfolio Limited Edition

Post Office Box 27
Napa, CA 94559
(707) 265-6555
www.portfoliowinery.com

Luc and Genevieve Janssens founded their winery in 1998. Genevieve was born to a French vintner family. She moved to California in 1979 to work at Robert Mondavi Winery as an assistant enologist and moved on to direct production at Opus One and then to direct wine-making at Robert Mondavi Winery. Luc was born in Brussels and is an artist and professor. Together they craft their Bordeaux-blend wine.

Portfolio 2002, Napa Valley, $120

One of the few wines at this price point whose price reflects its quality.

Full-bodied, dry.

Sweet oak, plum, cassis, rhubarb, basil, mint, and licorice notes. Full and lively with bright acidity and chewy tannins. Balanced, elegant, and complex. Delicious with roasted stuffed pork loin with garlic-jus.

Silver Horse Vineyards

2995 Pleasant Road
San Miguel, CA 93451
(805) 467-WINE
www.silverhorse.com

The Kroener family operated Silver Horse Vineyard and Winery from a converted barn from 1996 until 2005, when their new hilltop facility was opened. They source most of their grapes from surrounding estate vineyards and strive to make wines that winemaker Steve Kroener describes as "100% food-friendly."

Silver Horse Vineyards Sage 2004, Paso Robles, $42

A unique 50% malbec and 50% petit verdot blend. 150 cases produced.

Full-bodied, dry.

Subtle cherry, black currant, banana, peppermint, saddle, and oak notes. Juicy, chewy, and gripping with a drying finish. Decant for aeration. Enjoy with braised short ribs or Port Salut cheese.

Sullivan Vineyards

1090 Galleron Road
Post Office Box G
Rutherford, CA 94573
(707) 963-9646
www.sullivanwine.com

Jim Sullivan, a graphic designer, and his wife JoAnna purchased their prime Rutherford property in 1972, inspired by nearby Beaulieu Vineyards and Inglenook. Today his oldest son, Sean, is general manager. Winemaker Philippe Langner trained under internationally reknowned and controversial winemaker Michel Rolland.

Sullivan Vineyards Red Ink 2003, Napa Valley, $25

Excellent value.

Full-bodied, dry.

Balanced, rich, and clean blend of merlot, cabernet sauvignon, cabernet franc and petite verdot with cherry, tree leaf, and blackcurrant notes. Vibrant with silky tannins and a long finish. Enjoy with a Colorado lamb burger, quinoa with roasted eggplant, tomatoes and porcinis, or with a sweet, salty, mellow Basque cheese such as Iraty.

Bedell North Fork LLC

36225 Main Road (Route 25)
Cutchogue, NY 11935
(631) 765-4168
www.bedellcellars.com

Owner Michael Lynne, Co-Chairman and Co-CEO of New Line Cinema, met founding winemaker Kip Bedell who had established the seven-acre Bedell Vineyards at the site of an old potato farm. He now oversees the 78-acre property along with winemaker John Irving Levenberg. Vineyard Manager Dave Thompson is a member of the board of the Long Island Sustainable Agriculture program.

Bedell Cellars Merlot Reserve 2001, North Fork of Long Island, New York, $18

Unique style.

Medium-bodied, dry.

Gamey and inviting with notes of cassis, smoke, and green bell pepper. Smooth and round. All components well-integrated. Enjoy this with veal ragout with cepes and sage, or ahi tuna steaks.

Burrell School Vineyards & Winery

24060 Summit Road
Los Gatos, CA 95033
(408) 353-6290
www.burrellschool.com

Owners David and Anne Moulton began developing this historic Santa Cruz Mountains estate in 1973. Lyman J. Burrell settled this rugged area in 1854. Winemaker David focuses on chardonnay, merlot, cabernet franc, syrah, and pinot noir.

Burrell School Vineyards Estate Merlot 2002, Santa Cruz Mountains, $26

A wine that reflects its origins.

Full-bodied, dry.

Black cherry, plum, mocha, and vanilla bean notes. Supple and smooth. Delicious as a cocktail or with braised beef.

Casa de Caballos Vineyards

2225 Raymond Avenue
Templeton, CA 93465
(805) 434-1687
www.casadecaballos.com

Tom and Sheila Morgan planted their first grapes on what was then known as Morgan Farms in 1981. Within a few years, their planting area had grown to about six acres, and they decided to bond and rename the winery. Today they raise Arabian horses alongside their grapes.

Casa de Caballos Merlot Ultraviolet 2003, Paso Robles, $26

Good value.

Medium-bodied, dry.

Well balanced and highly structured, this wine has rich dark berry and licorice notes and a long, spicy finish. Pairs well with beef and vegetable stew.

Cathedral Ridge Winery

4200 Post Canyon Drive
Hood River, OR 97031
(541) 386-2882
www.cathedralridgewinery.com

Owned by Robb Bell, Cathedral Ridge Winery (formerly Flerchinger Vineyards) is located in an area of Oregon known for beautiful views and awesome windsurfing as well as for premium wine. The winemaker is Mike Sebastiani.

Cathedral Ridge Merlot 2004, Columbia Gorge, Oregon, $20

Intense, mature, and well balanced.

Full-bodied, dry

Aromas of red berries, blackberries, leather, and oak. Spicy, yet soft and lingering on the palate, with a rich finish. Try it with roasted lamb chops and potatoes with a brandy mustard sauce.

College Cellars of Walla Walla

500 Tausick Way
Walla Walla, WA 99362
(509) 524-5170
www.collegecellars.com

College Cellars of Walla Walla, the only two-year teaching commercial winery in the U.S., is primarily run by students, who make the wines to put their studies into practice. Bonded in 2003, the winery produces about 1200 cases per year.

College Cellars Merlot Klipsun Vineyard 2003, Red Mountain, Washington, $22

Made by student winemakers, but tastes like it could have been made by professionals.

Full-bodied, dry.

Mildly fruity nose. Notes of blackberry jam and chocolate. Round, velvety mouth-feel and a long, berry-rich finish. Delicious with butter-basted grilled white salmon steaks.

Darcie Kent Vineyards

7639 Cedar Mountain Drive
Livermore Valley, CA 94550
(925) 443-5368
www.darciekentvineyards.com

Proprietors Darcie and David Kent sought conditions similar to those in Pomerol, the area in Bordeaux, France, where merlot thrives, and settled on the Livermore Valley, part of the San Francisco Bay American Viticultural Area (AVA). They also produce estate-grown olive oil.

Darcie Kent Vineyards Merlot 2003, Livermore Valley, $24

A serious, cellar-worthy wine. Excellent value. 150 cases produced.

Full-bodied, dry.

Sweet, jammy boysenberry and mulberry notes and well-integrated sweet oak tannins. Thick, mouth-filling texture. Decanting is recommended. Serve with pappardelle with braised rabbit or truffled quail.

Delectus Winery

908 Enterprise Way, Suite C
Napa, CA 94558
(707) 255-1252
www.delectuswinery.com

Owner and winemaker Gerhard Reisacher, an eighth-generation wine-maker who grew up in a small village near Vienna, Austria, tasted Napa Valley wines for the first time as a college student. He was so impressed that he packed up his belongings and moved there. He and his wife launched Delectus in 1995.

Delectus Dog-Gone Good 2002, Napa Valley, $45

This Napa merlot is priced at about half and is twice as good as many of its competitors.

Full-bodied, dry.

This merlot-based blend is smooth, opulent, and juicy with tar, cherry, blueberry, sandalwood and cinnamon notes, and a pleasant chewy, mouth-gripping sensation. Delicious with sirloin steak with maitre'd butter, pork tenderloin with pomegranate sauce, or with Emmentaler cheese.

JM Cellars

14404 137th Place Northeast
Woodinville, WA 98072
(206) 321-0052
www.jmcellars.com

JM Cellars is a family-owned winery located on the "Bramble Bump," just above Chateau St. Michelle in Woodinville, Washington. Owner and winemaker John Bigelow learned from one of the best—Mike Januik of Januik winery.

JM Cellars Merlot Klipsun and Ciel du Cheval Vineyards 2003, Red Mountain, Washington, $32

A big merlot from two of Washington's premier vineyards. Only 120 cases produced.

Full-bodied, dry.

Rich and fruity, with flavors of cherry, raspberry and butterscotch, and a long, rich finish. Tastes great with fresh, crunchy sourdough bread and chicken marsala.

Lowden Hills Winery

535 Northeast Spitzenburg Road
College Place, WA 99324
(509) 527-1040
www.lowdenhillswinery.com

Owned and operated by Jim and Sonja Henderson, Lowden Hills Winery is located in a big red barn that dates back to 1938. Jim is a self-taught winemaker whose love for the vine led him to open the winery and take classes at U.C. Davis to learn more about the craft.

Lowden Hills Merlot Win Chester Vineyard 2003, Walla Walla Valley, Washington, $24

Good value.

Medium-bodied, dry.

Mouth-watering with blueberry, cherry, vanilla, hazelnut, and bell pepper notes. Try it with a mushroom risotto or a wood-fired white mushroom pizza.

Lucero Vineyards & Winery

10654 Texas Hill Road
Post Office Box 244
Dobbins, CA 95935
(530) 692-9214
www.lucerovineyards.com

In 1996, Dan and Marian Lucero and their four daughters planted their vineyard on former cattle-grazing land that was in their family since 1906. Cabernet sauvignon, merlot, and chardonnay are their focus.

Lucero Vineyards Merlot Reserve 2003, Sierra Foothills, $16

Very polished. Good value.

Full-bodied, dry.

Plum, fig, vanilla, cedar, and tar notes. Soft and slightly chewy. Enjoy with duck confit or pulled pork.

McCray Ridge

Post Office Box 1402
19400 McCray Ridge Road
Healdsburg, CA 95448
(707) 869-3147
www.mccrayridge.com

In 1972, owners Stan and Julie Simpson, reknowned for their single vineyard merlot, left behind their cushy life in Laguna Beach and camped in a trailer while having plumbing, electricity, wells, and phone lines put into the 40-acre parcel they fell in love with in the backroads of Sonoma. Today they focus on mountain grown merlot and cabernet sauvignon.

McCray Ridge Merlot Two Moon Vineyard 2002, Dry Creek Valley, $20

Excellent value.

Medium-bodied, dry.

Earth, mint, mocha, and tar notes. Smooth, luscious palate with sour cherry fruit and a slightly bitter aftertaste. Julie recommends this with her "Meatloaf Bourgoignon."

Mountain Spirit Winery

16150 Country Road 220
Salida, CO 81201
(719) 539-7848
www.mountainspiritwinery.com

Located on five acres in Colorado's Upper Arkansas Valley and surrounded by fruit orchards, the Mountain Spirit Winery specializes in *vinifera*-fruit blends. The results are often surprisingly delicious—something different, as owner Terry Barkett and her co-vintner Mike Barkett say.

Mountain Spirit Winery Merlot/Raspberry 2004, Upper Arkansas River Valley, Colorado, $13

Unique blend of 90% merlot and 10% raspberry wine.

Light-bodied, off-dry.

Fresh and fruity, with flavors of raspberry and blueberry. The perfect complement to Sunday brunch or a summery spinach salad with goat cheese and a raspberry vinaigrette.

Old Creek Ranch Winery

10024 Old Creek Road
Oakview, CA 93022
(805) 649-4132
www.oldcreekranch.com

Owned and managed by John and Carmel Whitman, Old Creek Ranch is what remains of a Spanish land grant awarded to Don Fernando Tico hundreds of years ago. Wine has been produced continually on the land since the late 1800s, and the original winery still stands.

Old Creek Ranch Merlot Rancho Sisquoc Vineyard 2003, Central Coast, $12

Unique style.

Full-bodied, dry.

Aromas of dark berries, leather, and licorice. Velvety-smooth, with rich blackberry, boysenberry, and molasses notes. Try it with an authentic spaghetti alla carbonara, or enjoy with some artisanal Scharffen Berger chocolate for dessert.

Palumbo Family Vineyard & Winery

40150 Barksdale Circle
Temecula, CA 92591
(951) 676-7900
www.palumbofamilyvineyards.com

Owner Nicholas Palumbo is a professional chef and produces about 1500 cases annually keeping in mind what foods the wines will go best with. Most of the estate vines are more than 10 years old.

Palumbo Family Winery Merlot Catfish Vineyard 2004, Temecula Valley, $34

Decadent style. 98 cases produced.

Full-bodied, dry.

Velvety and richly flavored with blackberry, vanilla, chocolate, and espresso notes. Long finish. Delicious with oven-roasted turkey and cranberry sauce.

Patrick M. Paul Vineyards

107 South 3rd Avenue
Walla Walla, WA 99362
(509) 526-0676
www.pmpvineyards.com

Owned and operated by Mike and Teresa Paul, Patrick M. Paul Vineyards began in 1984 with a small planting of cabernet franc. They have kept their production extremely limited over the years, now producing only 350 cases per year of cabernet franc, cabernet sauvignon, and merlot.

Patrick M. Paul Merlot 2003, Walla Walla Valley, Washington, $21

Intense, but highly approachable.

Full-bodied, dry.

Richly aromatic, with notes of blackberry, currant, vanilla, and toasty oak. Medium tannins, moderate acid, and a long finish. Try it with a hearty kielbasa and red potato soup.

Piety Flats Winery

2560 Donald-Wapato Road
Wapato, WA 98951
(509) 877-3115
www.pietyflatswinery.com

In 2001, Partners Bryan Eglet and Jim Russi reopened Donald Fruit and Mercantile, which was originally opened in 1911, to serve as a general store. When they met Willow Crest's winemaker Dave Minick, the idea to turn the general store into Piety Flats Winery was born.

Piety Flats Merlot 2002, Yakima Valley, $17

Great value; a fine cocktail-hour wine.

Light-bodied, dry.

Soft blackberry, raspberry, and plum notes. Silky-smooth mouth-feel, with a long, slightly spicy finish. Excellent with braised beef pot roast, carrots, and potatoes.

Raphael

Road Route 25
Peconic, New York, 11958
(631) 765-1100
www.raphaelwine.com

John Petrocelli established this winery in 1996 and named it after his father. The 60-acre vineyard is located on a gentle slope overlooking the Peconic Bay, just 2000 feet away. Looking to the great Bordeaux wines for inspiration, Petrocelli hired consulting enologist Paul Pontallier, of Chateau Margaux. Sustainable farming and hand harvesting are practiced.

Raphael Merlot 2001, North Fork of Long Island, New York, $30

A ringer for Bordeaux and reasonably priced.

Full-bodied, dry.

Tar, cassis, blueberry, pencil shavings, tobacco, and hay notes. Smooth and supple with fine-grain tannins and a long finish. Very understated and elegant. Serve with rack of lamb, spring lamb chops, or with filet mignon.

Robinson Family Vineyards

5880 Silverado Trail
Napa, CA 94558
(707) 944-8004
www.robinsonfamilyvineyards.com

Third generation family members continue to own and operate the winery started by their grandfather, Norman Robinson. Nathan Fay and Father Tom Turnbull were early mentors.

Robinson Family Vineyards Merlot Estate Grown 2003, Stag's Leap District—Napa Valley, $39

Unique style.

Medium-bodied, dry.

Strawberry, plum, vanilla, and pink rose notes. Smooth and supple with an unusual undercurrent of white peach. Delicious with roast chicken or grilled duck breast.

Rosenthal—The Malibu Estate

29000 Newton Canyon Road
Malibu, CA 90265
(310) 463-9532
www.rosenthalestatewines.com

George Rosenthal planted vineyards at his 250-acre Malibu estate in 1987, after having owned hotels and movies studios for a number of years. Winemaker is Christian Roguenant, whose credits include a stint as winemaker and president of Laetitia Winery.

Rosenthal Merlot Devon Vineyard 2001, Malibu— Newton Canyon, $25

Good value.

Full-bodied, dry.

Black cherry, plum, and olive notes on the nose. Flavors of black cherry, chocolate, and toasted oak. Rich, intense, and supple. Pairs well with broiled T-bone steak and sweet shallots.

Six Hands Winery

13783 Isleton Road
Post Office Box 444
Walnut Grove, CA 95690
(916) 776-2053
www.sixhandswinery.com

Owner Peter Marks has a wine heritage going back several generations. His great-grandfather, Joseph Machado, farmed the land here and his grandfather Bill Guerard taught him the art of winemaking. With his degree from U.C. Davis in Plant Sciences and Enology, and his wife Richele's expertise in genetics, the couple realized the natural potential of the Delta and set up their winery on the family's century-old ranch.

Six Hands Merlot Yolo Vineyards 2003, Dunnigan Hills, $10

Good value.

Full-bodied, dry.

Dust, mineral, wet stone, cherry, raspberry, pencil lead, and tobacco notes. Light oak and balanced acids. Elegant Bordeaux-like texture and structure. Enjoy with sliced roast beef.

Suncé Winery

1839 Olivet Road
Santa Rosa, CA 95401
(707) 526-9463
www.suncewinery.com

Croatian native Dr. Frane Franicevic and his wife Janae purchased
the winery in 1998 and named it Suncé, or "sun" in Croatian. They
produce a wide variety of reds and whites from top vineyards in both
Sonoma and Lake Counties.

Suncé Winery Merlot Hedin Vineyard 2004, Russian River Valley, $35

Unique style.

Full-bodied, dry.

Cranberry, cherry, raisin, and white pepper notes. Appealing fruity,
peppery palate with bright acidity for excellent food compatibility.
Enjoy with empanadas or with Port Salut cheese.

Temptress Wines

2517 Northwest 83rd Place
Portland, OR 97229
(503) 730-9633
www.temptresswines.com

Based in McMinnville, Oregon, Temptress Wines produces only two
varietals: merlot and pinot noir. Winemaker Laurent Montalieu was
brought up in the French winemaking tradition, taking his first steps
in a Medoc vineyard owned by his great-grandfather and attending
high school in Bordeaux.

Temptress Merlot 2000, Rogue Valley, Oregon, $20

Elegant, expressive, and enticing.

Full-bodied, dry.

Earthy and spicy, with black cherry, cassis, and leather notes. Round,
velvety mouth-feel. Long, rich finish. Delicious with breaded pork
tenderloin or with chicken fried steak.

Willis Hall

4715 126th Street Northeast
Marysville, WA 98271
(360) 653-1247
www.willishall.com

Winemaker and owner John Bell, a former employee of the Boeing Company, retired in 2004 to begin making wine full time. A largely self-taught winemaker, his experience comes from years of interest in wine and what he learned as a member of the Boeing Wine Club.

Willis Hall Merlot 2003, Columbia Valley, Washington, $26

Good varietal expression.

Medium-bodied, dry.

Cherry cola, plum, blackberry jam, black pepper, and molasses notes. Try with spit-roasted chicken basted in rosemary and garlic butter.

Scott Aaron Wines

2225 Raymond Avenue
Templeton, CA 93465
(805) 434-1687
www.scottaaron.com

Scott Aaron says that he learned everything he knows about wine
from his father, Tom Morgan, proprietor of Casa de Caballos Vineyards.
He currently produces extremely limited quantities of cabernet franc
and viognier— only two or three barrels each— and markets them
exclusively through his website and the Casa de Caballos tasting room.

Scott Aaron Cabernet Franc Blend (cabernet franc, merlot, and cabernet sauvignon) Integrity 2003, Paso Robles, $55

Unforgettable. 93 cases produced.

Full-bodied, dry.

Aromas of cloves, leather, and blackberries. Complex and layered, with
notes of dark berries, leather, smoke, and very smooth tannins. Try it
with slow-roasted brisket.

Broad Run Vineyards

10601 Broad Run Road
Louisville, KY 40299
(502) 231-0372
www.broadrunvineyards.com

Broad Run Vineyards began in 1983 as an experiment to see what
varietals would grow well in Kentucky soil. Pleased with the results,
the Kushner-Hyatt family went commercial in 1992, releasing their first
vintage in 1994. Broad Run was officially bonded in 2003. All their
grapes are estate-grown.

Broad Run Cabernet Sauvignon Reserve 2002, Ohio River Valley, Kentucky, $20

Mature and well-crafted.

Full-bodied, dry.

Ripe cherry, blackberry, and spice notes with medium tannins and mild, well balanced acidity. Rich, velvety mouth-feel and a long finish. Excellent with broiled steak in Gorgonzola-walnut sauce.

Cooper-Garrod Estate Vineyards

22645 Garrod Road
Saratoga, CA 95070
(408) 867-7116
www.cgv.com

Manager and winemaker George Cooper and vineyard manager Jan Garrod, along with members of both families, own and operate this 28-acre estate. They produce chardonnay, viognier, syrah, cabernet franc, and cabernet sauvignon.

Cooper-Garrod Cabernet Franc Francville Vineyard 2003, Santa Cruz Mountains, $24

Modeled after a Loire Valley Chinon, the light, drinkable wine found often in Parisian cafés.

Medium-bodied, dry.

Cherry, raisin, spearmint, Asian five-spice, and tart cranberry notes. Lush fruit, soft oak tannins, and vivid acidity. Enjoy with grilled dark meat chicken or turkey.

Detert Family Vineyards

1746 Vineyard Avenue
St. Helena, CA 94574
(877) 817-0466
www.detert.com

Oakville winegrowers since 1953, the Detert Family quietly provided their estate-grown fruit to some of the Napa Valley's most famous wineries, including Robert Mondavi and Opus One. They launched their own label in 2000, and produce limited quantities of cabernet franc.

Detert Family Cabernet Franc 2003, Napa Valley, $45

This is one of the best values in Napa Valley premium red wine. Only 200 cases produced.

Full-bodied, dry.

Cabernet franc typically plays a supporting role in Bordeaux blends, but is allowed to shine here, giving its characteristic bright cherry notes along with the more cabernet sauvignon-like cassis, leaf, tobacco, and spice notes. Distinct fruit and mineral characteristics are a signature of this wine. Delicious with subtle, classic dishes such as beef Wellington or wild mushroom mille feuille.

Giessinger Winery

365 Santa Clara Street
Fillmore, CA 93015
(805) 494-1122
www.giessingerwinery.com

Giessinger Winery was born in a converted welder's shop near Fillmore's train depot in 1997. Owner and winemaker Eduoard Giessinger teaches wine tasting classes at U.C. Santa Barbara. The winery also offers older reserves, such as the 97 zinfandel, at excellent values.

Giessinger Cabernet Franc 2001, Lodi, $30

Excellent and hard to find. One of the few 100% cabernet francs made in California.

Medium-bodied, dry.

Robust and mature, with dark berry, oak and black pepper notes, and a lingering finish. Delicious with onion-brazed short ribs and spinach roulade.

Lucchesi Vineyards & Winery

19698 View Forever Lane
Grass Valley, CA 95945
(530) 273-1596
www.lucchesivineyards.com

Owners Mario and Linda Clough established their winery in 2002, while planting of the steeply terraced mountain vineyards began in

1999. Their "View Forever Vineyard" overlooks Nevada County from the snow-capped Sierra to the Sacramento basin. Heather Nenow is winemaker. Matt Wentz is Vineyard Manager.

Lucchesi Cabernet Franc 2003, Sierra Foothills, $24

One of the more complex versions of this wine in America. Good value.

Full-bodied, dry.

Wild mountain herb, sage, mint, green tea, cherry, violet, and earth notes. Lush, velvety texture with low acid and well-integrated oak. Very silky tannins. Enjoy with grilled flank steak or pork loin with rosemary and sage dressing.

Naked Mountain Vineyard

2747 Leeds Manor Road
Post Office Box 115
Markham, VA 22643
(540) 364-1609
www.nakedmtn.com

Bob and Phoebe Harper were amateur winemakers for years before they bought some property in the Blue Ridge Mountains of Virginia and planted their own *vinifera* grapes in 1976. Though they had intended for the vineyard to be just a hobby, it quickly grew into a commercial venture. The winery, established in 1981, now produces about 5000 cases per year of *vinifera* table wines, specializing in chardonnay.

Naked Mountain Cabernet Franc 2004, Virginia, $20

Unique style.

Full-bodied, dry.

Smooth, supple mouth-feel, with cherry, toasted oak and leather notes, and soft tannins. Try it with garlic creamed chicken served over your favorite pasta.

Napa Redwoods Estate

4723 Redwood Road
Napa, CA 94558
(707) 226-1800
www.naparedwoods.com

Owners Michael and Lynn Yates grow all their own grapes on their family ranch on Mt. Veeder, in the hills between Napa and Sonoma. The famous Castle Rock Vineyard from preprohibition days is on their property.

Napa Redwood Estate Cabernet Franc 2002, Mt. Veeder—Napa Valley, $38

One of a handful of producers of single varietal cabernet franc. 150 cases made.

Full-bodied, dry.

Like a big, juicy cabernet sauvignon, but with cherry rather than cassis notes and a tart, mouth-watering finish. Delicious with beef tenderloin with scallion butter, meatloaf, or wild mushroom black pepper pasta.

Patrick M. Paul Vineyards

107 South 3rd Avenue
Walla Walla, WA 99362
(509) 526-0676
www.pmpvineyards.com

Owned and operated by Mike and Teresa Paul, Patrick M. Paul Vineyards began in 1984 with a small planting of cabernet franc. They have kept their production extremely limited over the years, now producing only 350 cases per year of cabernet franc, cabernet sauvignon, and merlot.

Patrick M. Paul Cabernet Franc Minnick Hills Vineyard 2004, Walla Walla Valley, Washington, $62

Excellent release from this veteran cabernet franc producer.

Medium-bodied, dry.

Subtle and silky-smooth on the palate, with black cherry, spice and tar notes, and a slightly oaky finish. Excellent with lasagna.

Vin de Tevis

51161 Covelo Road
Dos Rios, Mendocino County, CA 95429
(707) 983-8433
www.vindetevis.com

Steve and Carol De Tevis produce a limited amount of unique red wine, including cabernet franc, merlot, cabernet sauvignon, pinot noir, and charbono from their remotely located vineyard in new American Viticultural Area (AVA), Dos Rios (granted in November 2005).

Vin de Tevis Cabernet Franc 2001, Mendocino County, $25

Unusual port-like style. 404 bottles produced.

Full-bodied, dry.

Fig, raisin, blackberry, almond, hazelnut, and caramel notes. Very rich and intense with sweet ripe fruit and chalky tannins. Enjoy this 17.3% alcohol wine after dinner with a cheese plate.

Allora Vineyards

Post Office Box 1008
St. Helena, CA 94574
(707) 963-1227
www.alloravineyards.com

Terry and Nancy Klein established Allora Vineyards in 1999, retiring
from their very successful plastering business to concentrate on
making small production, high quality wine. Consulting winemaker
Rudy Zuidema of Robert Craig Wine Cellars and Wirra Wirra Winery
in Australia continue to work primarily with cabernet sauvignon.

Allora Lusso Cabernet Sauvignon 2003, Napa Valley, $100

At this audacious price, most Napa Valley wines are massive and
overwrought. This is a refreshing change of pace.

Full-bodied, dry. 115 cases produced.

Cranberry, boysenberry, blueberry, raisin, date mission fig, and mint
notes. Full, round, soft, and creamy with vibrant fruit and a juicy
finish. Delicious with venison and mustard sauce or as an after-dinner
"wine of meditation."

Avio Vineyards

14520 Ridge Road
Sutter Creek, CA 95685
(209) 267-1515
www.aviowine.com

After 9/11 Stefano and Lisa Watson wanted a change of lifestyle (he
lost two colleagues and decided he didn't want to be flying as much).
They visited winemaking uncles in Avio near Lake Garda and Tuscany,
Italy, and then began their search for their property. They fell in love
with the rolling hills of Amador County and the small town atmos-
phere, which reminded them of Italy, so they set up shop and have
been focusing on Italian varietals ever since. Sustainable and organic
farming are practiced.

Avio Vineyards Cabernet Sauvignon 2002, Amador County, $28

Unique style.

Full-bodied, dry.

Mocha, cocoa, raisin, and plum notes. Warm and ripe with a silky center and a dark bitter chocolate/cherry finish. Delicious with braised pork tenderloins.

Benjamin Silver Wines

1318 East Mason Street
Santa Barbara, CA 93103
(805) 963-3052
www.silverwine.com

Owned by Benjamin Silver, one of Santa Barbara's "up-and-coming" young winemakers. Benjamin Silver Wines produces extremely limited quantities of red varietals and viognier.

Silver Wines Cabernet Sauvignon Casa Blanca Vineyard 2001, Santa Barbara County, $30

An excellent Santa Barbara expression of the varietal.

Medium-bodied, dry.

Aromas of cherry, plum, vanilla, and pine. Highly complex, with flavors of dark berries, white pepper and hay, and a long, spicy finish. Delicious with sliced turkey breast and cherry sauce.

Black Coyote Wines

2400 Third Avenue
Napa, CA 94558
(707) 252-2292
www.blackcoyotewines.com

Two doctors and their hospital services colleagues, Dr. Bates, Dr. Olin Robison, Jack Ruffle, and Stanley Trotman, merged their talents and resources to form Black Coyote Wines, where they produce only chardonnay and cabernet sauvignon. Art Finkelstein of Judd's Hill is winemaker.

Black Coyote Cabernet Sauvignon Bates Creek Vineyard 2003, Stag's Leap District—Napa Valley, $32

Excellent varietal expression. Good value.

Full-bodied, dry.

Vibrant fruit notes of boysenberry, cassis, and sour dark cherry meld with creamy, vanillan oak notes. Slightly chewy palate. Bold style but beautifully integrated oak, alcohol, and acid components. Seamless. The owners recommend it with barbecue pulled pork.

Broman Cellars

945 Deer Park Road
St. Helena, CA 94574
(800) 514-4401
www.bromancellars.com

Owner and winemaker Bob Broman worked with Stag's Leap Wine Cellars, Concannon Vineyards, St. Supery, and Guenoc before launching his own label in 1994. He produces a cabernet sauvignon, sauvignon blanc, and syrah.

Broman Cabernet Sauvignon 2001, Napa Valley, $48

Elegant, understated style. 727 cases made.

Full-bodied, dry.

Plum tart, raisin, cassis, tar, earth, cedar chest, and pine notes. Supple and smooth. Well balanced. Enjoy with chestnut-stuffed game hen.

Chanticleer

4 Vineyard View Drive
Yountville, CA 94599
(707) 945-0566
www.chanticleerwine.com

George and Cadd Grodahl, owners of the Morningside Vineyard, wanted to make a Super-Tuscan style wine, blending just a touch of

sangiovese into their cabernet sauvignon. After meeting Chris Dearden, winemaker at Benessere Vineyards—an Italian varietal specialist—he decided to partner with him to produce Chanticleer.

Chanticleer Cabernet Sauvignon 2003, Yountville—Napa Valley, $47

A fully ripe Napa cab without the harsh tannins. 438 cases produced.

Full-bodied, dry.

Silky, voluptuous tannins and a brooding, earthy, bitter cherry character. The partners recommend this with chicken with sweet red peppers, steak au poivre, striped bass wrapped in Serrano ham, and potato and wild mushroom gratin with blue cheese.

Chateau Faire Le Pont

389 Technology Center Way
Wenatchee, WA 98801
(509) 670-0422
www.fairelepont.com

Located in a renovated 1920s brick warehouse, Chateau Faire Le Pont produces 3000 cases a year from Yakima Valley, Alderdale, and Mattawa grapes. Doug and Debé Brazil founded the winery in 2004, fulfilling a lifelong dream of Doug, a former Navy helicopter pilot. They encourage wine lovers to learn about wine firsthand through their "adopt-a-vine program."

Chateau Faire Le Pont Cabernet Sauvignon Elerding 2003, Yakima Valley, Washington, $33

Lush, fruit-forward style.

Full-bodied, dry.

Plush and complex, with layers of currant, black cherry and chocolate, and a fragrant nose of raisin and spice notes. Long and slightly spicy finish. Try it with veal cutlets or a Philly cheese steak sandwich.

Chateau Margene

4385 La Panza Road
Creston, CA 93432
(805) 238-2321
www.chateaumargene.com

Established in 1998, Chateau Margene produces about 2000 cases per year of cabernet sauvignon, cabernet franc, petit verdot, and merlot. The winery is owned and operated by winemaker Michael Mooney and his family.

Chateau Margene Cabernet Sauvignon 2003, Paso Robles, $38

Ripe, fruit-forward style.

Full-bodied, dry.

Aromas of cedar, currant, and black pepper. Robust and chewy, with blackberry, boysenberry, cola, and oak notes. Enjoy with rack of lamb and garlic mashed potatoes, or with a juicy cheeseburger and fries.

Corison Winery

987 St. Helena Highway
St. Helena, CA 94574
(707) 963-9826
www.corison.com

Winemaker Cathy Corison and her husband William Martin are partners in the business too. With a B.A. in Biology from Pomona College in Claremont, California, an M.S. in Enology from U.C. Davis, and 30 years of winemaking for others, including a decade at Chappellet Vineyard, she decided to venture off on her own. Her estated vineyard, Kronos Vineyard, is farmed organically.

Corison Winery Cabernet Sauvignon 2002, Napa Valley, $58

Built to last. A classic.

Full-bodied, dry.

Subtle cassis, cherry, blueberry, pencil shavings, and wild mountain

herb notes. Silky and round with a slightly chewy aftertaste. Oak is beautifully integrated. Delicious with roasted pork loin, daube of beef provencale, or crepes champignons.

Devitt

11412 Highway 238
Jacksonville, OR 97530
(541) 899-7511
www.devittwinery.com

After having owned Pope Valley Winery in Napa Valley for 15 years, owner and winemaker James Devitt took a hiatus from the wine business in the mid-80s. He returned and opened Devitt in 2001, focusing mostly on red varietals as well as viognier and chardonnay.

Devitt Cabernet Sauvignon Estate Bottled 2003, Rogue Valley, Oregon, $24

An excellent Oregon cabernet sauvignon. Fairly priced.

Medium-bodied, dry.

Aromas of pepper, blueberry, oak, and vanilla. Subtle and smooth on the palate, with notes of black pepper, cherry, and vanilla. Pair with game such as rabbit stew with bacon and shallots or consider a cassoulet.

D.R. Stephens Estate

1860 Howell Mountain Road
St. Helena, CA 94574
(707) 963-2908
www.drstephenswines.com

Owners Don and Trish Stephens planted their nine-acre vineyard in 1996 and released their first wine in 2002 with the help of winemaker Celia Welch Masyczek and vineyard manager Jim Barbour. Their son, Justin Hunnicutt Stephens, is general manager. Don is still active in his legal career and with his real estate and private equity investment business.

D.R. Stephens Cabernet Sauvignon Moose Valley Vineyard 2002, Napa Valley, $100

Up and coming. 1054 cases produced.

Full-bodied, dry.

Cassis, blueberry, raspberry, espresso, mocha, vanilla, and nutmeg notes. Rich and plummy with supple tannins. Enjoy with a bacon-wrapped veal loin.

Dutcher Crossing Winery

8533 Dry Creek Road
Post Office Box 53
Healdsburg, CA 95448
(707) 431-2700
www.dutchercrossingwinery.com

Bruce Nevins and Jim Stevens co-founded Perrier North America and worked together in wine distribution before partnering to launch their Dutcher Crossing Winery. Stevens, former CCO of Coca Cola, purchased 35 acres in 2001, partnered with Nevins, and hired Kerry Damskey as winemaker.

Dutcher Crossing Cabernet Sauvignon Proprietors Reserve 2003, Dry Creek Valley, $25

A blend of 75% cabernet sauvignon and 25% syrah.

Full-bodied, dry.

Cherry, plum, cassis, fig, date, and vanilla notes. Smooth, supple, and polished with very luscious fruit and well-integrated oak tannins and flavors. Enjoy with rib eye steak, muscovy duck breast, or faro with porcini mushrooms.

Dyer Straits Wine Company

1501 Diamond Mountain Road
Calistoga, CA 94515
(707) 942-5502
www.dyerwine.com

Bill and Dawnine Dyer (she was winemaker for 25 years at Domaine Chandon, he spent 20 years as Sterling Vineyards winemaker) planted 2.2 acres of cabernet sauvignon on their 12-acre parcel in 1993.

Dyer Cabernet Sauvignon 2002, Diamond Mountain District—Napa Valley, $70

A polished, elegant, understated style. 250 cases produced.

Full-bodied, dry.

Cassis, fresh mountain air, cherry, and tar notes. Full, soft texture with fine tannins, subtle fruit, and a long, bright, lively finish. Decant for best results (for aeration, not sediment). Delicious with roast beef or with almond crusted lamb chops with foie gras and truffles.

Eagle's Trace

680 Rossi Road
St. Helena, CA 94574
(707) 963-4412
www.eaglestrace.com

Owner Gus Anderson worked first as a home winemaker then studied winemaking and grape growing at U.C. Davis. His 26 acres in Con Valley receive cooling breezes each afternoon from nearby Lake Hennessy, allowing for a longer, slower growing season.

Eagle's Trace Cabernet Sauvignon 2003, Napa Valley, $75

Opulent, but very well balanced.

Full-bodied, dry.

Cedar, cassis, and tar notes. Rich, supple, and smooth with vivid underlying acidity and a long, flavorful finish. Delicious with braised shortribs with horseradish crust or flank steak bordelaise.

Fantesca Estate Winery

2920 Spring Mountain Road
St. Helena, CA 94574
(707) 968-9229
www.fantesca.com

When Caroline Bale married Charles Krug in 1860 this estate was her dowry. Current owners Duane and Susan Hoff, along with winemakers Nils Venge and his son Kirk focus on premium cabernet sauvignon. A chardonnay is also produced.

Fantesca Estate Winery Cabernet Sauvignon 2002, Spring Mountain District — Napa Valley, $60

Varietally expressive and unique.

Full-bodied, dry.

Tar, tobacco, cassis, and cherry notes with a funky undercurrent. Juicy, vibrant, mouth-filling palate with pleasant, grippy Spring Mountain tannins. Delicious with prime rib or lamb shank.

Frazier Winery

40 Lupine Hill Road
Napa, CA 94558
(707) 255-3444
www.frazierwinery.com

Owner Bill Frazier was a commercial pilot for United Airlines for over 30 years. In 1990, he planted grapes on the Lupine Hill Estate and opened Frazier Winery in 1995. He and his family focus on cabernet sauvignon, merlot, petit verdot, and cabernet franc. John Gibson of Chappellet, Stag's Leap Wine Cellars, and Vine Cliff Winery is winemaker.

Frazier Memento Cabernet Sauvignon 2003, Napa Valley, $95

Full-blown style with balance.

Full-bodied, dry.

As this wine opens with air it shows notes of earth, boysenberry, apple brandy, and sweet oak. With high alcohol and low acidity it is very rich, but still manages to retain balance. Long, chewy, bitter cherry finish. Enjoy with grilled lamb chops with balsamic mushroom sauce.

Grape Ranch Vineyards

Rural Route 3, Box 198C
Okemah, OK 74859
(918) 623-2250
www.graperanch.com

Owned by Dan and Jack Whiteman and their families, Grape Ranch Vineyards harvested its first fruit in 2005. Currently, they source their grapes from vineyards around the nation. The largest winery in Oklahoma, they host numerous events such as the annual Woodie Guthrie Festival.

Grape Ranch Cabernet Sauvignon Festivus 2003, Sonoma County, $16

A good Sonoma County cabernet sauvignon via Oklahoma Sooner country.

Full-bodied, dry.

Spicy, earthy aromas, with black pepper, leather, and dark fruit notes. Medium oak tannins are well balanced with firm acids. Excellent with beef tips and onions simmered in a balsamic reduction.

Hagen Heights

1184 Hagen Road
Napa, CA 94558
(707) 226-2634
www.hagenheights.com

D.J. and Diane Smith's first release, their 2002 cabernet sauvignon, is already garnering critical acclaim. Located in the southeastern end of Napa Valley, the cooler climate allows for two to three weeks longer hang time, or ripening of the grapes. Mike Wolf was vineyard construction manager. Heather Pyle is winemaker, and Raul Gloria is vineyard manager.

Hagen Heights Cabernet Sauvignon 2002, Napa Valley, $48

Top notch first release. 250 cases produced.

Full-bodied, dry.

Baked fruit, mission fig, mulberry, tar, and vanilla notes. Smooth and supple with excellent varietal character on the finish. Decant and serve with roast rack of lamb.

hope & grace

Beard Plaza
6540 Washington Street
Yountville, CA 94599
(707) 944-2500
www.hopeandgracewines.com

Owner and winemaker Charles Hendricks named his winery after his two daughters. Since the early 1980s he has worked with Viader, Barnett, Regusci, Paoletti, Bacio Divino, and Stelzner. Today he focuses on pinot noir from Monterey and a Napa Valley cabernet sauvignon, and will release shortly a Napa Valley chardonnay and malbec.

hope & grace Cabernet Sauvignon 2003, Napa Valley, $45

Lavishly oaked, but with understated fruit for balance.
450 cases produced.

Full-bodied, dry.

Dark and earthy with cassis, lilac, wet tree bark, nutmeg, mint, and basil notes. Smooth, creamy texture turns chewy as oak tannins kick in. Slightly drying finish. Decant for aeration. Enjoy with a grilled porterhouse steak or a creamy, ripe Camembert cheese.

Hopper Creek Winery

6204 Washington Street
Napa, CA 94558
(707) 944-2139
www.hoppercreek.com

Owner Dieter Tede, a native of Germany, has family ties to the wine
industry as far back as the 1860s. Today he oversees both Hopper
Creek and Audobon Cellars and has recently hired winemaker
Barry Grushkowitz.

Hopper Creek Winery Cabernet Sauvignon Los Chamizal Vineyards 2002, Sonoma Valley, $45

Excellent varietal expression for such a ripe style.

Full-bodied, dry.

Plum, cassis, bitter cherry, fig, and raspberry jam notes. Mouth-filling
with well-integrated oak tannins. Tart finish. Delicious with garlic
rubbed steak with sea salt and chunky black peppercorns.

Horizon Cellars

466 Vineyard Ridge
Siler City, NC 27344
(919) 523-9463
www.horizoncellars.com

Designed by owner and self-taught winemaker Guy Loeffler, Horizon
Cellars was bonded in 2003 after Guy decided to make a career
change from his former position at Hewlett-Packard. About half of his
grapes are estate-grown and he sources the others from Chatham
County growers.

Horizon Cellars Cabernet Sauvignon 2004, Piedmont Region, North Carolina, $19

Big, bold style.

Full-bodied, dry.

Spicy aromas with underlying fruit notes of blackberry, cassis, and
plum. Rich and chewy, with dark berry, spice, and Dr. Pepper notes.
Delicious with seared pork chops and cranberry dressing.

Hourglass Vineyard

1104 Adams Street, Suite 103
St. Helena, CA 94574
(707) 968-9332
www.hourglasswines.com

Proprietor Jeff Smith's father Ned purchased this six-acre vineyard and
planted four acres to zinfandel in 1976. After phylloxera devastated
the vineyard, Jeff learned they were in the "pinch" of the hourglass,
or narrowest point in Napa Valley, and replanted with heat-loving
cabernet sauvignon. Every afternoon the wind picks up in this unique
microclimate, cooling the vines and slowing the ripening process.
Consulting winemaker Bob Foley crafts deeply flavored, complex
wines from this top notch vineyard.

Hourglass Cabernet Sauvignon 2003, Napa Valley, $110

Benchmark wine. 700 cases produced.

Full-bodied, dry.

Vanilla bean, caramel, mocha, tar, black licorice, menthol, and cassis
notes. Bold, intense, mouth-coating style with ripe fruit and lavish oak,
but all components are well-integrated. Delicious with standing rib roast
au jus.

Hunnicutt

2611 Colombard Court
St. Helena, CA 94574
(707) 963-2908
www.drstephenswines.com

Justin Hunnicutt Stephens, son of D.R. Stephens Estate Wines founder
and proprietor Don Stephens, left his career in commercial real estate
to work in the wine business. Starting from the ground up, he worked
at Miner Vineyards, Saddleback Cellars, and Seavey Vineyards before
joining the family business in 2004. He is now general manager for
both D.R. Stephens and his own label, Hunnicutt.

Hunnicutt Cabernet Sauvignon 2004, Napa Valley, $39

Good value. 325 cases produced.

Full-bodied, dry.

Cassis, cranberry, raspberry, red licorice, tar, and vanilla notes. Seamless and elegant. Enjoy with wild salmon a la plancha with a cabernet reduction.

Judd's Hill

2332 Silverado Trail
Napa, CA 94558
(707) 963-9093
www.juddshill.com

Art and Bunnie Finkelstein and their son, Judd and his wife Holly are the team behind Judd's Hill. Art gave up his job as an architect and his wife gave up teaching. They moved from Los Angeles to Napa and have been making wine ever since, most notably founding Whitehall Lane in the '70s. Judd is taking over the reins as winemaker these days.

Judd's Hill Cabernet Sauvignon 2002, Napa Valley, $42

Classic, traditional-style Napa cab that shines with food.

Medium-bodied, dry.

Currant, tobacco, and oak notes. Smooth, ripe tannins. Tart acids give balance and lift. The winery recommends enjoying this wine with steaks, spicy poultry dishes, cheddar or blue cheese, barbequed ribs and other red meats, and Italian-influenced dishes.

Kathryn Kennedy Winery

13180 Pierce Road
Saratoga, CA 95070-4212
www.kathrynkennedywinery.com

Kathryn Kennedy planted her eight-acre Santa Cruz Mountains vineyard to cabernet sauvignon in 1973 after graduating from U.C. Davis and speaking with locals. Her youngest son, Marty Mathis, became winemaker in 1981. Today he and his wife reside at the winery. The wines are known for their intense character and ageability. Sustainable farming is practiced.

Kathryn Kennedy Estate Cabernet Sauvignon 2002, Santa Cruz Mountains, $125

Benchmark wine.

Full-bodied, dry.

Closed at first, the wine opens up with notes of plum, cassis, earth, tar, tobacco, and spice. This multi-dimensional wine is rich in flavor and has chewy, mouth-filling fruit tannins and subtle, well-integrated oak tannins. Decant and serve with veal chops or lamb.

Little Vineyards Family Winery

15188 Sonoma Highway
Glen Ellen, CA 95448
(707) 477-6298
www.littlevineyards.com

In 1996, Joan and Rich Little purchased a 25-acre property from the Hanford Family in Glen Ellen. Joan's brother, Ted Coleman, is winemaker and partner along with his wife Rachel. Their winery was bonded in 2000 and their first two releases were the 2002 zinfandel and the 2002 Resonance, a syrah/cabernet sauvignon blend. Today they also produce the Band Blend—Rich Little plays in a band—as well as a cabernet sauvignon.

Little Vineyards Cabernet Sauvignon, Sonoma Valley, $40

Varietal character really shines through. 257 cases produced.

Medium-bodied, dry.

Cassis, cherry, plum, pencil shaving, tobacco, wet stone, leafy, and musky notes. Decadent, round entry becomes chewy and gripping with slightly drying oak tannins picking up towards the finish. Decant for aeration. Enjoy with beef Wellington.

Lowden Hills Winery

535 Northeast Spitzenburg Street
College Place, WA 99324
(509) 527-1040
www.lowdenhillswinery.com

Owned and operated by Jim and Sonja Henderson, Lowden Hills
Winery is located in a big red barn that dates back to 1938. Jim is
a self-taught winemaker whose love for the vine led him to open the
winery and take classes at U.C. Davis to learn more about the craft.

Lowden Hills Cabernet Sauvignon Pepper Bridge Vineyard 2003, Walla Walla Valley, Oregon, $27

Rich and beautifully structured.

Medium-bodied, dry.

Aromas of black cherry, currant, leather, and black olives, with cherry
and spice notes on the palate. Decanting recommended. Try it with
mushroom-stuffed pork chops and green beans.

Marston Family Vineyard

Post Office Box 668
St. Helena, CA 94574
(707) 963-8490
www.marstonfamilyvineyard.com

The 400-acre mountainside vineyard (of which about 10% is planted)
of Michael and Alexandra Marston was first planted in the late 1890s.
Winemaker Philippe Melka, of Chateau Petrus in France and Dominus
in Napa Valley, focuses on cabernet sauvignon, merlot, and syrah.

Marston Family Vineyard Cabernet Sauvignon 2002, Spring Mountain District—Napa Valley, $80

Excellent expression of Spring Mountain "terroir." 500 cases produced.

Full-bodied, dry.

Bold ripe berry, rhubarb, green olive, tomato, vanilla, maple, and molasses notes. Fairly aggressive fruit and oak tannins give chewiness and structure. Decant or age to soften. Enjoy with grilled sirloin steak with green peppercorn mustard sauce.

Meander Cellars

Post Office Box 146
St. Helena, CA 94574
(707) 963-3773
www.meanderwines.com

Amy Aiken followed her then boyfriend Joel to Napa Valley with her masters in plant pathology from U.C. Santa Cruz. During her first wine country interview (with Craig Williams at Joseph Phelps Vineyards) she was given the brush off. When finally in exasperation she dropped Joel's name—he was then and still is winemaker at Beaulieu Vineyards—she was hired on the spot. She produces exclusively this 100% cabernet sauvignon.

Meander Cabernet Sauvignon 2003, Napa Valley, $65

Outstanding first release. 200 cases made.

Full-bodied, dry.

Mint, hay, earth, boysenberry, framboise, currant, mission fig, clove, espresso, and red rose petal notes. Opulently fruity palate restrained by fruit and oak tannins. Toasted oak slightly drying on the finish. Decant for aeration. Enjoy with a grilled porterhouse steak.

Mettler Family Vineyards

Post Office Box 403
Victor, CA 95253
(888) 509-5969
www.mettlerwine.com

With 100-year-old vineyard properties and eight generations of wine industry experience, the Mettler family is a force in Lodi. They were one of the first families to introduce French clones here. Organic and biologically integrated farming systems are in place to insure the highest quality fruit.

Mettler Family Vineyards Cabernet Sauvignon Estate Vineyard 2002, Lodi, $22

A very unique, old vine, warm-climate expression. Good value.

Full-bodied, dry.

Ripe baked fruits with raisin and fig notes. Balanced with bright, juicy acidity, and chewy tannins. The family recommends this with short ribs with cabernet and porcini mushrooms, barbequed lamb chops with fresh rosemary, fillet medallions and caramelized onions, and dark chocolate.

Midsummer Cellars

107 Lilac Lane
St. Helena, CA 94574
(707) 967-0432
www.midsummercellars.com

Winemaker and owners Rollie and Sally Heitz focus on cabernet sauvignon from their Canon Creek Vineyard and from the half-acre Mann Vineyard in the heart of Rutherford, which was in the hands of close family friends up until recently.

Midsummer Cellars Cabernet Sauvignon Mann Vineyard 2003, Napa Valley, $35

Very balanced and accessible style. 131 cases produced.

Medium-bodied, dry.

Very accessible plum and blackcurrant notes with moderate alcohol and oak. Pleasant underlying acidity and a tart black currant aftertaste. Delicious with loin of pork with huckleberry reduction, or braised lentils with eggplant and mushroom.

Alexandria Nicole Cellars

2880 Lee Road
Prosser, WA 99350
(509) 786-3497
www.alexandrianicolecellars.com

On the bluffs overlooking the Columbia River in Washington State,
former Assistant Viticulturalist for Hogue Cellars, Jarrod Boyle planted
the first vines of his estate vineyard, Destiny Ridge, in 1998. He then
went on to found Alexandria Nicole Cellars, where he produces about
4800 cases a year of 15 different varietals.

Alexandria Nicole Cabernet Sauvignon Destiny Ridge Vineyards 2003, Columbia Valley, Washington, $30

First release from the estate vineyard.

Medium-bodied, dry.

Aromas of dark fruit and spices. Black currant, jam, spice, and leather
notes. Rich and velvety on the palate, with medium tannins and
refreshing acids. Excellent with venison medallions in balsamic
reduction, or try with a roast beef sandwich.

Olive Hill Lane Press

2995 Woodside Road, Suite 400
Woodside, CA 94062
(866) 473-1761
www.olivehilllanepress.com

Cliff Jurnigan makes just a few barrels a year of 100% cabernet
sauvignon from a three-acre estate in Woodside. He uses the same
oak barrels as Chateau Mouton-Rothschild in Bordeaux.

Olive Hill Cabernet Sauvignon 2005, $40

Early 2007 release. 48 cases produced.

Full-bodied, dry.

Barrel sample tasted. Young and somewhat reclusive with currant,
blueberry, unique oak spice, and bell pepper notes. Very chewy and

grippy. Should come together nicely by time of release. Enjoy with a grilled veal chop.

Palmaz Vineyards

4029 Hagen Road
Napa, CA 94558
(707) 226-5587
www.palmazvineyards.com

Amalia Palmaz purchased the famous Cedar Knoll Vineyard of Henry Hagen—it had been shut down in prohibition and never reopened—with her husband in 1997. Winemaker Tina Mitchell and Vineyard Manager Fernando Trejo, along with consulting winemaker Mia Klein and consulting Vineyard Manager Mike Wolf, focus on cabernet sauvignon. Sustainable farming is practiced on the 29 acres of vineyards.

Palmaz Vineyards Cabernet Sauvignon 2002, Napa Valley, $100

Up and coming. 720 cases produced.

Full-bodied, dry.

Cassis, currant, plum, black licorice, and cinnamon notes. Smooth and supple with ripe fruit and slightly drying oak tannins. Decant for aeration. Enjoy with venison or a rib-eye steak.

Paradise Ridge

4545 Thomas Lake Harris Drive
Santa Rosa, CA 95403
(707) 528-9463
www.paradiseridgewinery.com

Walter Byck married Marike Hoenselaars 41 years ago in Holland. They discovered "paradise," 156 acres of it, in 1965, and today, the family produces sauvignon blanc, syrah, zinfandel, and cabernet sauvignon.

Paradise Ridge Cabernet Sauvignon Rockpile Vineyard 2002, Sonoma County, $33

Good value.

Full-bodied, dry.

Tar, mocha, earth, oak, and plum notes with chalky tannins and a long, plummy finish. Enjoy with grilled London broil with chile-olive dip.

Piña Napa Valley

8060 Silverado Trail
Napa, CA 94558
(707) 738-9328
www.pinanapavalley.com

As sixth generation Napa Valley farmers, the Piña family has access to some of the best fruit around. They built their winery in 1981, and released their first cabernet sauvignon in 2000. Ted Osborne is winemaker. The family focuses on 100% cabernet sauvignon wines.

Piña Cabernet Sauvignon Estate Grown 2003, Howell Mountain—Napa Valley, $66

Excellent expression of origin and varietal.

Full-bodied, dry.

Cedar chest, cinnamon sticks, mulberry, mineral, and tar notes. Firm mountain tannins with a long plumy, rhubarb finish. Enjoy with Peruvian skirt steak or aged Jack cheese.

Revana Family Vineyards

2930 St. Helena Highway North
St. Helena, CA 94574
(707) 967-8814
www.revanawine.com

While visiting the Napa Valley in 1997, Dr. Madaiah Revana, a practicing cardiologist out of Houston, discovered a small parcel of prime vineyard land just north of the town of St. Helena and purchased it. He brought in vineyard manager Jim Barbour and winemaker Heidi Peterson Barrett to bring his vision of crafting world class cabernet sauvignon to life. Tom Garrett is general manager.

Revana Family Vineyards Cabernet Sauvignon 2002, Napa Valley, $90

A very high caliber wine for such a new venture. 2000 cases produced.

Full-bodied, dry.

Cassis, red licorice, vanilla, cedar, and cherry cobbler notes. Smooth, round, and rich with Barrett's signature soft, ripe tannins. Long flavorful finish. Delicious with sirloin steak with herb butter.

Saint Laurent Winery

4147 Hamlin Road
Malaga, WA 98828
(509) 888-9463
www.saintlaurent.net

Michael and Laura Laurent Mrachek started their career as fruit growers with a few acres of cherries in 1978. They now farm merlot, syrah, and cabernet sauvignon on 260 acres in Columbia Valley.

Saint Laurent Cabernet Sauvignon 2003, Columbia Valley, Washington, $14

An outstanding value.

Medium-bodied, dry.

Powerfully fruity nose dominated by aromas of blackberry, currant, and vanilla. Subtle, with well balanced acids, smooth tannins, and mild vanilla, raisin, and tea notes. Pairs well with roast duck or meats high in fat.

Saucelito Canyon Vineyard

3180 Biddle Ranch Road
San Luis Obispo, CA 93401
(805) 543-2111
www.saucelitocanyon.com

William and Nancy Greenough purchased the Saucelito Canyon property in 1974. They produced their first vintage in 1982 and now release about 2500 cases per year of zinfandel, cabernet sauvignon, tempranillo, and sauvignon blanc.

Saucelito Canyon Cabernet Sauvignon 2004, Arroyo Grande Valley, $20

Excellent Southern California cabernet sauvignon. Good value.

Medium-bodied, dry.

Rich aromas of lavender, roses, blueberry, and spice. Dark berry, leather, and vanilla notes, with a long, slightly oaky finish. Pairs well with simple grilled meats and vegetables.

The Vineyard at Strawberry Ridge

23 Strawberry Ridge Road
Warren, CT 06754
(860) 868-0730
www.strawberryridge.com

Proprietors Susan and Robert Summer were inspired by their trips to Tuscany and Chianti in the 1980s to open their own vineyard on 22 acres of hilly Connecticut countryside in 1992. Their full production of cabernet and chardonnay, from vines over 10 years old, is harvested and crafted by hand.

Strawberry Ridge Cabernet Sauvignon Ascot Reserve 2003, USA, $38

West Coast grapes meet East Coast style. A blend of grapes from both Connecticut and 75-year-old California vines.

Full-bodied, dry.

Full and supple, with dark berry, currant, pepper, vanilla, and tar notes. Long, spicy finish. Decanting recommended. Great with corned beef roast or a Reuben sandwich.

Sullivan Vineyards

1090 Galleron Road
Post Office Box G
Rutherford, CA 94573
(707) 963-9646
www.sullivanwine.com

Jim Sullivan, a graphic designer, and his wife JoAnna purchased their prime Rutherford property in 1972, inspired by nearby Beaulieu Vineyards and Inglenook. Today his oldest son, Sean, is general manager. Winemaker Philippe Langner trained under flying winemaker Michel Rolland.

Sullivan Vineyards Cabernet Sauvignon 2003, Rutherford — Napa Valley, $55

Unusual and distinctive style.

Medium-bodied, dry.

Sweet oak, earth, saddle, Asian five-spice, cassis, plum, and cherry notes. Chewy and bold with an edge of funk like a traditional southern Italian red. Delicious with braised lamb shanks with roasted plums, arrosto misto (pit-roasted sausage and lamb), or with seitan and shiitake mushroom stroganoff.

Terra Valentine

3787 Spring Mountain Road
St. Helena, CA 94574
(707) 967-8340
www.terravalentine.com

Owners Angus and Margaret Wurtele moved to Napa Valley to retire
and start a small winery. They purchased hillside vineyards on Spring
Mountain. Angus brings a wealth of experience with a Stanford
Business School degree and a 34-year career with his family business,
Valspar Corporation. Margaret brings experience in writing, publishing,
and philanthropy to the table. Together with general manager and
winemaker Sam Baxter they concentrate on Spring Mountain cabernet
sauvignon along with Cal-Ital blends and pinot noir.

Terra Valentine Cabernet Sauvignon 2002, Spring Mountain District—Napa Valley, $35

Polished and elegant with very fine tannins for a mountain-grown
cabernet sauvignon. Excellent value.

Full-bodied, dry

Dried cherry, prune, blueberry, green and pink peppercorn, and nutmeg
notes. Very smooth and layered with plum and spice notes. Long,
expressive finish. Enjoy with pappardelle with roasted duck and
wild mushrooms.

Terra Valentine Cabernet Sauvignon Wurtele Vineyard 2002, Spring Mountain District—Napa Valley, $50

Very high caliber. Could easily sell for twice the price.

Full-bodied, dry

Pine tree, soft berry, cassis, poivre vert (green peppercorn), picholine
and lucques olive, leafy, mint tea, pencil lead, and vanilla bean notes.
Smooth and supple with layers of flavors, vibrant varietal expression,
and a long, expressive finish. Enjoy with steak Diane.

Amphora Winery

4791 Dry Creek Road, Building 6
Healdsburg, CA 95448
(707) 431-7767
www.amphorawines.com

Winemaker and co-owner Rick Hutchinson combines his love of pottery and winemaking at the winery named after those vessels used to store and transport wine in Greek and Roman times. In 1997, the "winery" was in the basement of a prune barn. In spring, 2006 they relocated to a larger space complete with artist studios to accommodate the growth to current levels of 3500 cases. From the original petite sirah, and zinfandel, Rick has expanded the line to include cabernet sauvignon, merlot, and syrah.

Amphora Zinfandel Mounts Creek Vineyard 2004, Dry Creek Valley, $24

Old-vine intensity. Good value.

Full-bodied, dry.

Raspberry, blueberry, spearmint, black licorice, and cinnamon notes. Decadently ripe and intense with smooth oak tannins. Well balanced. Winemaker Rick Hutchinson recommends wild mushroom bisque, beef stew, or even a flourless chocolate cake.

Auriga Wine Cellars

3500 Carson Road #D2
Camino, CA 95709
(530) 647-8078
www.aurigawines.com

Named after the "charioteer," a constellation in the Northern hemisphere, Auriga Wine Cellars is located in El Dorado County and all wines come from vineyards in the Sierra Foothills, famous for the gold rush.

Auriga Cellars Zinfandel 2002, El Dorado County, $15

One of a kind and a great price.

Full-bodied, dry.

Maple, pine cone, boysenberry, raspberry, date, and cinnamon notes. Subtle for this type of zinfandel with a pleasing texture and a slightly drying finish. Delicious with ancho chile pulled pork, and the winery recommends steaks with chipotle butter.

Bella Luna Winery

1850 Templeton Road
Templeton, CA 93465
(805) 434-5477
www.bellalunawine.com

Founder Kevin Healey has a 30-year history in the winemaking business, while his partner, Sherman Smoot, is a former commercial aviator and self-taught winemaker. They focus on Italian varietals, particularly sangiovese.

Bella Luna Fighter Pilot Red (85% zinfandel, 10% sangiovese, 5% cabernet sauvignon) 2003, Paso Robles, $30

Tastes almost identical to a fine version of its Italian sibling, primitivo.

Medium-bodied, dry.

Delicate aromas of wild berries, violet, and bay leaf, with blackberry, licorice, and basil notes. Delicious with a summery green bean, chicken, and almond casserole.

Calcareous Vineyard

3430 Peachy Canyon Road
Paso Robles, CA 93446
(805) 975-6541
www.calcareous.com

After selling his wine and beer distributing business in Sioux City, Iowa, Lloyd Messer moved out to Paso Robles and established the 442-acre Calcareous Vineyard in 2000. His daughter, Dana Brown, also sold her Iowa wine distributing business and joined him with her little sister Erika, making this a rare father-daughter run winery. Justin Kahler is the winemaker.

Calcareous Zinfandel 2003, Paso Robles, $24

Big, powerful style. Good value.

Full-bodied, dry.

Intense, port-like aromas of blackberry jam, cocoa, and oak. Powerful and rich, with blackberry, anise and spice notes, and a long, enticing finish. Try it with wild mushroom beef stew.

Cantiga Wineworks

Post Office Box 66
Somerset, CA 95684
(530) 621-1696
www.cantigawine.com

Rich and Christine Rorden founded their Sierra Foothills winery with the help of family and friends. Their philosophy is old-fashioned and not trendy—to produce balanced wines that are ageworthy and that are ideal to enjoy with food. Farming is with minimal intervention.

Cantiga Wineworks Zinfandel Tim & Edie's Vineyard 2001, Sierra Foothills, $21

It is nice to be able to purchase a slighty older wine.
265 cases produced.

Full-bodied, dry.

Sweet port-like nose and palate with blueberry and chocolate layer cake notes. Big-boned but balanced with a fluffy, seductive texture. The Rorden's recommend it with roasted, grilled or smoked pork, chicken or venison, anything with sun-dried tomatoes, kalamata and green olives, or dishes seasoned with tomato BBQ sauces, balsamic vinegar, or savory plum or berry sauces or glazes.

Deaver Vineyards

12455 Steiner Road
Shenandoah Valley
Plymouth, CA 95669
(209) 245-4099
www.deavervineyards.com

Owner Ken Deaver oversees a ranch with 300 acres of vines planted as far back as 1853 by his great-grandfather. Today the vineyard still has 120-year-old zinfandel vines that were in the past sold to home winemakers. Today the winery focuses on this old-vine zinfandel along with sangiovese, barbera, and ports.

Deaver Vineyard Zinfandel 2003, Amador County, $37

Benchmark wine.

Full-bodied, dry.

Decadently fruity with raspberry, mulberry, and strawberry notes. Very soft, lush palate with baked fruit notes, oak tannins, and juicy acidity. Long cranberry-imbued finish. The Deaver's recommend coq au vin Deaver style or roasted leg of lamb with gravy.

Dover Canyon Winery

4520 Vineyard Drive
Paso Robles, CA 93446
(805) 237-0101
www.dovercanyon.com

Owner and winemaker Dan Panico, former winemaker for Eberle Winery, has been making wine for 17 years. He started producing his own in 1992 while still at Eberle. Mary Baker, former director of the Paso Robles Wine Country Alliance, does marketing and helps on the crush pad and in the vineyard. Dover Canyon is a certified wildlife habitat.

Dover Canyon Old Vine Zinfandel 2004, Central Coast, $27

100% zinfandel from 80-year-old vines.

Full-bodied, dry.

Aromas of plum, blackberry, black pepper, and dust. Complex and subtle palate, with raspberry, pepper, plum, and smoke notes. Enjoy with an open-faced turkey sandwich and mashed potatoes.

Dutcher Crossing Winery

8533 Dry Creek Road
Post Office Box 53
Healdsburg, CA 95448
(707) 431-2700
www.dutchercrossingwinery.com

Bruce Nevins and Jim Stevens co-founded Perrier North America and worked together in wine distribution before partnering to launch their Dutcher Crossing Winery. Stevens, former CCO of Coca Cola, purchased 35 acres in 2001, partnered with Nevins, and hired Kerry Damskey as winemaker.

Dutcher Crossing Zinfandel Maple Vineyard 2004, Dry Creek Valley, $34

A hybrid style combining richness and ripeness with an understated elegance.

Full-bodied, dry.

Boysenberry, cassis, earth, mocha, dust, and dark bitter chocolate notes. Very balanced with a long, expressive finish. Enjoy with BBQ tri-tip (without the sweet sauce) or roasted pork.

Dutton-Goldfield Winery

825 Gravenstein Highway North, Suite 3
Sebastopol, CA 95472
(707) 823-3887
www.duttongoldfield.com

In 1998, Steve Dutton of the famous Dutton family of grape growers, now in their third generation, partnered with longtime colleague and friend Dan Goldfield to produce the style of refreshing, food friendly wines they would enjoy at home. While their cool-climate Green Valley (a sub-appellation of Russian River Valley) pinot noirs are some of the best in America, they also produce a few hundred cases of zinfandels which are worth seeking out.

Dutton-Goldfield Zinfandel Morelli Lane 2004, Green Valley—Russian River Valley, $40

Old-vine intensity. Benchmark wine.

Medium-bodied, dry.

Sweet ripe raspberry and blueberry, milk chocolate, lily, and fresh forest notes. Deeply flavored and intense. Smooth and luscious with well-integrated oak tannins and balancing acidity. The winery recommends enjoying this with grilled steak or swordfish, or assertive cheeses.

Esterlina Vineyards

1200 Holmes Ranch Road
Post Office Box 2
Philo, CA 95466
(707) 895-2920
www.esterlinavineyards.com

For several generations the Sterling family has been producing small lots of handcrafted wines from some of California's best vineyards. Today production centers around grapes grown in the family's estate vineyards including the American Viticultural Area (AVA), Cole Ranch.

Esterlina Bacigalupi Vineyards Zinfandel 2003, Russian River Valley, $25

Time capsule selection. This is what American wine is all about.

Full-bodied, dry.

Ripe and opulent with blackberry, cranberry, dark chocolate, and vanilla flavors juxtaposed with the bright, juicy acidity and perfume of California's gorgeous Russian River Valley. Serve with burgers topped with a crust of Point Reyes Blue (Marin County, California), grilled skirt steak wrapped in bacon, pork chops with wasabi mashed potatoes, or crispy duck.

Fanucchi Vineyards

Post Office Box 290
Fulton, CA 95439
(707) 526-3219
www.fanucchivineyards.com

Peter Fanucchi began his career in wine in 1972, working alongside his father in the vineyard and winery crafting traditional wines mainly from century-old zinfandel vines. In 1992, he started his own label using fruit from the Fanucchi Wood Road Vineyard (sustainable farming is practiced). Today his old-vine zinfandel as well as trousseau gris, an aromatic white, are highly sought after by those in the know.

Fanucchi Vineyards Old Vine Zinfandel The Fanucchi Wood Road Vineyard 2002, Russian River Valley, $36

Excellent varietal character. Old-vine intensity.

Full-bodied, dry.

Soft perfume and a deeply fruited core of boysenberry, framboise, and banana. Silky, seductive texture with a refreshing, juicy aftertaste. Delicious with a grilled burger topped with melted blue cheese, or a cheese plate with Gouda, sharp cheddar, and Emmentaler.

Hendry Wines

3104 Redwood Road
Napa, CA 94558
(707) 226-8320
www.hendrywines.com

Former Agronomy professor George Whiting Hendry and his wife Margaret purchased the 117-acre Hendry Ranch in 1939. Along with partner Susan Ridley, sales and marketing manager, and Mike Hendry, George's nephew, the team focuses on lot-specific zinfandels from over 50 vineyard blocks on the property.

Hendry Block 7 Zinfandel 2004, Napa Valley, $28

Old-vine intensity.

Full-bodied, dry.

Intoxicating late season berries, cherry cobbler, cassis, framboise, mint, violet candy, and vanilla bean notes. Ripe and bold with an oaky finish. Enjoy with barbecued baby back ribs with mustard sauce.

Hendry Block 28 Zinfandel 2002, Napa Valley, $31

Carmen Miranda meets John Wayne.

Full-bodied, dry.

Front loaded with enticing perfume, cassis, blueberry, currant, decadently ripe raspberries, and dark chocolate, this wine has almost port-like richness of fruit but is bone dry, well-structured and has vibrant underlying acidity for balance. Delicious with zinfandel marinated pot roast, Roquefort-wild mushroom fondue, or cassoulet.

The Hobo Wine Company

10295 Westside Road
Healdsburg, CA 95448
(707) 887-0833
www.hobowines.com

Kenny Likitprakong of Thailand who owns Banyan wines with his father Somchai launched his own label in 2002. Total production is about 500 cases per year.

Hobo Zinfandel 2004, Russian River Valley, $20

Big-boned but not flashy or trendy.

Full-bodied, dry.

Subtle notes of Italian black licorice, earth, and boysenberry pie. Very smooth and viscous with fine-grain tannins and firm acidity. Delicious with steak au poivre vert or miso-glazed wild rice tempeh.

Victor Hugo Vineyards

2850 El Pomar Drive
Templeton, CA 93465
(805) 434-1128
www.victorhugowinery.com

Owner and winemaker Victor Hugo Roberts started his career in the wine industry in 1982 after getting his degree in enology from U.C. Davis. He and his wife Leslie planted their first grapes in 1985 and soon began to make wines in a 100-year-old barn on their land in Templeton.

Victor Hugo Zinfandel 2004, Paso Robles, $18

Good value.

Full-bodied, dry.

Lush aromas of dark berries, oak, and tar. Layers of blackberry, currant, and black pepper notes. Pairs well with beef tenderloin with bourbon and brown sugar glaze, or with other bold meats.

Kaz Vineyard & Winery

233 Adobe Canyon Road
Post Office Box 1190
Kenwood, CA 95452
(707) 833-2536
www.kazwinery.com

Winemaker and owner Richard Kasmier, a.k.a. Kaz, his wife, Sandi, and their two children, Ryan and Kristen oversee every detail, including creating the labels, ads, and website. They farm and produce organic wine and specialize in unique red blends, rare varietals, and ports.

Kaz "Zam" Pagani Ranch Vineyards 2002, Sonoma Valley, $65

Unique 100-year-old vine "field blend." A taste of vinous history.

Full-bodied, dry.

This blend of 80% zinfandel, 15% alicante bouchet, and 5% mourvedre has rich cedar, maple, mission fig, plum, and cherry notes with

freshly ground black pepper and nutmeg on the long, spicy finish.
Enjoy with lamb shank, mustard-crusted venison, or Port Salut cheese.

Muccigrosso Vineyards

21450 Bear Creek Road
Los Gatos, CA 95033
(408) 354-0821
www.muccigrosso.com

Michael and Lynn Muccigrosso planted their vineyards on their Santa
Cruz Mountain property in the 1980s. With Jacob Kauffman as
winemaker and CEO David Agretelis, they concentrate on estate-grown
pinot noir, zinfandel, and a Super-Tuscan blend of syrah, sangiovese,
cabernet sauvignon, and petite sirah.

Muccigrosso Vineyards Lyn Zin Zinfandel 2003, Monterey County, $20

Richly fruited but not excessively high in alcohol or oak tannins.

Full-bodied, dry.

Jammy and ripe with notes of boysenberry, mulberry, raspberry, cassis,
orange zest, oak spice, and cigar box. Boldly flavored. Smooth and
balanced. Enjoy with grilled meats, vegetables, or fish with black
cherry barbecue sauce.

Nadeau Family Vintners

3860 Peachy Canyon Road
Paso Robles, CA 93446
(805) 239-3574
www.nadeaufamilyvintners.com

Self-proclaimed "mavericks," Robert and Patrice Nadeau of Nadeau
Family Vintners produce about 2500 cases per year of big, flavorful
red wines. The winery, which was established in 1997, is located four
miles east of Paso Robles and holds tastings inside their combination
tasting room and wine making laboratory.

Nadeau Zinfandel Epic 2003, Paso Robles, $28

Benchmark zinfandel for Paso Robles. Only 177 cases made.

Full-bodied, dry.

Rich aromas of raspberry and pine. Opulent and powerful, yet exceptionally smooth, with notes of blackberry jam, vanilla, and smooth, round tannins. Delicious with portobello mushrooms baked with Gorgonzola cheese.

Paradise Ridge

4545 Thomas Lake Harris Drive
Santa Rosa, CA 95403
(707) 528-9463
www.paradiseridgewinery.com

Walter Byck married Marike Hoenselaars 41 years ago in Holland. They discovered "paradise," 156 acres of it, in 1965 and today the family produces sauvignon blanc, syrah, zinfandel, and cabernet sauvignon.

Paradise Ridge Zinfandel Hoenselaars Vineyard 2003, Russian River Valley, $30

Super-ripe style but without the trendy over-use of heavily toasted oak.

Full-bodied, dry.

Vanilla, boysenberry, and Australian black licorice notes. Heft from oak but very well-integrated and lifted with zesty acidity. Long, cherry cola finish. Try with habanero/anchovy marinated BBQ ribs, well-seared steak, or fajitas.

Saucelito Canyon Vineyard

3080 Biddle Ranch Road
San Luis Obispo, CA 93401
(805) 543-2111
www.saucelitocanyon.com

William and Nancy Greenough purchased the Saucelito Canyon property in 1974. They produced their first vintage in 1982 and now release about 2500 cases per year of zinfandel, cabernet sauvignon, tempranillo, and sauvignon blanc. Saucelito Canyon is home to some of the oldest zinfandel vines in California, some dating to the 1880s.

Saucelito Canyon Zinfandel 2004, Arroyo Grande Valley, $20

A great example of the quintessential American wine.

Medium-bodied, dry.

Highly aromatic, with notes of cherry, blueberry, boysenberry, and dust. Smooth, creamy mouth-feel, with spicy notes of black pepper and cloves, soft tannins, and a long finish. Try it with marinated goose breasts or enjoy with a handful of cashews.

Storybook Mountain Vineyards

3835 Highway 128
Calistoga, CA 94515
(707) 942-5310
www.storybookwines.com

Owners Jerry and Sigrid Seps named their winery in honor of the founders, the Brothers Grimm of fairy tale fame. Zinfandel is their specialty, much of it old vine, organically farmed, and crafted in a traditional "claret" or restrained, food friendly style.

Storybook Mountain Zinfandel Mayacamas Range 2003, Napa Valley, $27.50

One of the few remaining producers of the understated "claret" style of zinfandel.

Full-bodied, dry.

Subtle blackberry, cherry, earth, tar, and mineral notes. Elegant and supple. Decant for aeration. Enjoy with duck sausages.

Storybook Mountain Napa Estate Eastern Exposures Zinfandel 2003, Napa Valley, $37

Benchmark wine. Old-vine intensity.

Full-bodied, dry.

Deep, smoky, and berry notes with a restrained, elegant palate, and a long, flavorful finish. Serve with beef tenderloin in mushroom/zinfandel reduction, cassoulet, or quinoa pilaf with Fontina cheese.

Suncé Winery

1839 Olivet Road
Santa Rosa, CA 95401
(707) 526-9463
www.suncewinery.com

Croatian native Dr. Frane Franicevic and his wife Janae purchased the winery in 1998 and named it Suncé, or "sun" in Croatian. They produce a wide variety of reds and whites from top vineyards in both Sonoma and Lake Counties.

Suncé Winery Zinfandel Old Vines Baker Vineyard 2004, Russian River Valley, $30

Old-vine complexity and quality.

Full-bodied, dry.

Boysenberry, cranberry, celery, carrot, V-8, cedar, toast, and toasted barrel notes. Big, fat, fruity, and layered with a chewy palate and a long, red-fruit imbued finish. Delicious with grilled sausages or aged Gouda cheese.

Turtle Creek Winery

Post Office Box 691
Lincoln, MA 01773
(781) 259-9976
www.turtlecreekwine.com

Proud to be considered a "garagiste"— a French term referring to very small, boutique winemakers who might make their wine in a garage, shed, or shack—Kipton Kumler produces about 500 cases per year of chardonnay, riesling, pinot noir, and cabernet franc.

Turtle Creek Zinfandel Wildwood Vineyards 2004, Amador County, $16

A bargain for a great zin. Fewer than 100 cases made.

Full-bodied, dry.

Rich and smoky, with notes of dark berries, raisins, and savory spices. Medium oak tannins are well balanced with mild acids. Try it with shepherd's pie or roast goose.

Vino Con Brio

7889 East Harney Lane
Lodi, CA 95420
(209) 369-5392
www.vinoconbrio.com

Mike and Renae Matson and their three adult children own and operate both the winery and Amorosa Inn and Gardens. With winemaker Paul Wofford, they concentrate on zinfandel, Rhone, and Italian varietals.

Vino Con Brio Matzin Old Vine Zinfandel Estate 2003, Lodi, $21

Old-vine intensity and character. Excellent value.

Full-bodied, dry.

Wild morello cherry, framboise, peppermint, banana, violet candy, and earthy notes. Soft, billowy texture with pure, precise flavors and a long, velvety, expressive finish. Delicious with St. Louis style ribs, braised and grilled oxtails, or Robiola cheese.

Zahtila Vineyards

2250 Lake County Highway
Calistoga, CA 94515
(707) 942-9251
www.zahtilavineyards.com

Since the 1999 launch, owner Laura Zahtila has been actively involved
in every aspect of her business. A career changer (she left Cisco
Systems in San Jose), today she and her team, vineyard manager
Placido Garcia and assistant winemaker and cellar master Ignacio
Blancas, focus exclusively on cabernet sauvignon and zinfandel.

Zahtila Zinfandel 2003, Dry Creek Valley, $20

Good value. 859 cases produced.

Full-bodied, dry.

Raspberry, rosebush, and mint notes. Creamy texture with soft tannins,
vivacious acidity, and a pleasant, gripping finish. Delicious with Point-
Reyes blue cheese-topped burger or pork tenderloin, or vegetarian
shish kebabs.

Vincent Arroyo

2361 Greenwood Avenue
Calistoga, CA 94515
(707) 942-6995
www.vincentarroyo.com

The very humble Vincent Arroyo is known as a petite sirah master, and today has such a loyal following for these dry and sweet versions along with his cabernet sauvignon and cabernet sauvignon/syrah/petite sirah blend, "Entrada," that he sells only consumer direct to his loyal customer base.

Vincent Arroyo Petite Sirah Port 2004, Napa Valley, 375ml, $22

Made with the top 20 barrels of petite sirah. Good value.

Full-bodied, sweet.

Chocolate, mocha, and lip-smacking, juicy berry notes. Grapey and complex at the same time. Uncomplicated elegance. Enjoy with dark, bittersweet chocolate, a cigar, or on its own.

Bodega Bay Portworks

233 Adobe Canyon Road
Post Office Box 1190
Kenwood, CA 95452
(707) 833-2536
www.bodegabayportworks.com

Bodega Bay Portworks is a second label for Kaz Vineyard and Winery, located in Kenwood at the heart of Sonoma Valley. Winemaker and owner Richard Kasmier, a.k.a. Kaz, his wife, Sandi, and their two children, Ryan and Kristen oversee every detail including creating the labels, ads, and website. They also run a "Bed and get your own damn breakfast."

Bodega Bay Portworks Pirates Reserve Chardonnay White Port, Sonoma Valley, 375ml, $25

A new experience in dessert wine. 192 cases of 375ml bottles produced.

Full-bodied, sweet, fortified.

Butter, caramel, amaretto, banana crème, hazelnut, apple, pear, and honey notes. Sweet and rich. Delicious with almond biscotti or drizzled over vanilla bean ice cream.

Deaver Vineyards

12455 Steiner Road
Shenandoah Valley
Plymouth, CA 95669
(209) 245-4099
www.deavervineyards.com

Owner Ken Deaver oversees a ranch with 300 acres of vines planted as far back as 1853 by his great-grandfather. Today the vineyard still has 120-year-old zinfandel vines that were in the past sold to home winemakers. Today the winery focuses on this old-vine zinfandel along with sangiovese, barbera, and ports.

Deaver Vineyard Port, California, 375ml, $18

Understated for an American dessert wine.

Full-bodied, sweet, fortified.

Cherry, bittersweet chocolate, cedar, maple syrup, and raisin notes. Zin-like flavors come out followed by a creamy framboise/vanilla finish. Enjoy with raspberry crème brûleé, chocolate pots du crème, or a caramel éclair.

Grands Amis

115 North School Street, Suite 5
Lodi, CA 95240
(209) 369-6805
www.grandsamis.com

Jonathan and Cathy Wetmore transitioned from managing vineyards to making wine. In 2002, they started their own winery and hired South African native J.C. van Staden as winemaker. Zinfandel, syrah, petite sirah, barbera, cabernet sauvignon, and port are produced.

Grands Amis "Great Friends" Syrah Port 2002, Lodi, 500ml, $27

Good value.

Full-bodied, sweet, fortified.

Sweet cherry, boysenberry, raspberry, Hershey's Extra Dark, Fernet, and wet tree leaf notes. Very unctuous and balanced with a long, fruity finish. Delicious with peanut butter cookie bar with bittersweet chocolate and almond slivers.

Haak Wine

6310 Avenue T
Santa Fe, TX 77510
(409) 925-1401
www.haakwine.com

Owner Raymond Haak, who has a background in electrical engineering, began growing grapes in 1969. It was not until 1994, however, that he and his wife Gladys decided to turn their hobby into a commercial operation. They now produce about 5000 cases a year in their Mediterranean-style winery, which offers "a taste of the old world in Galveston County."

Haak Vintage Port 2002, Texas Gulf Coast Region, Texas, $17

A chocolate lover's choice.

Full-bodied, sweet.

Rich and chocolaty, with aromas of caramel and raisins. Smooth on the palate, with cherry, chocolate, and cinnamon notes. Excellent with warm orange spice cake or try it with homemade brownies.

Horizon Cellars

466 Vineyard Ridge
Silver City, NC 27344
(919) 742-1404
www.horizoncellars.com

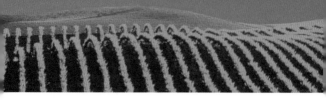

Designed by self-taught winemaker Guy Loeffler, Horizon Cellars was bonded in 2003 after Guy decided to make a career change from his former position at Hewlett-Packard. He grows about half his grapes and sources the others from Chatham County growers.

Horizon Cellars Sweet Blanc Carolina Comfort (49% chardonnay, 49% gewürztraminer, 2% muscat concentrate) 2004, Piedmont Region, North Carolina, $14

A unique blend with Southern flair.

Light-bodied, sweet.

Aromas of rose petals, citrus, and kumquat. Melon and fig notes, with crisp acidity and a sweet finish. Delicious with summer strawberries and crème fraîche.

Lenora Winery

632 Main Street
Ramona, CA 92065
(760) 788-1388
www.ramonavintnerscellars.com

Lenora Muscat of Alexandria 2003, Ramona Valley—San Diego County, 375ml, $8

Self-taught Swedish winemaker Frank Karlsson learned how to make wine firsthand in his own Ramona Valley vineyards. In 2001, he and his wife Kerstine went commercial with Lenora Winery. They now produce over a dozen varietals from their estate and other vineyards in the Ramona Valley area.

Great value.

Medium-bodied, sweet.

Aromas of pear, apple, and a hint of orange blossom. The palate is smooth and sweet with golden apple and honey notes. Delicious with warm fruit compote topped with vanilla ice cream.

Mokelumne Glen

8441 East Schmiedt Road
Lodi, CA 95240
(209) 369-5755
www.mokelumneglen.com

From grape growing to home winemaking in the 1970s, and now, to producing wine commercially, this third generation family specializes in German varietals. They practice sustainable farming.

Mokelumne Glen Dreirebe Select Late Harvest 2004, Lodi, $20

Outstanding value.

Medium-bodied, sweet.

This blend of three ("drei") grapes has pineapple, mango, guava, honey, apple brandy, roasting marshmallow, butter, and floral notes. Silky and honeyed with vivacious underlying acidity for balance. Delicious with passionfruit truffles.

Niagara Landing Wine Cellars

4434 Van Dusen Road
Lockport (Cambria), NY 14094
(716) 433-8405
www.niagaralanding.com

The land on which Niagara Landing rests has been in the Smith family since 1932. Peter and Nancy Smith, along with Mike and Jackie Connolly and Gary and Lori Hoover, now own and operate the winery. Some of the vines date to the late 1800s.

Niagara Landing Late Harvest Vidal, Finger Lakes, New York, 750ml, $12

Good value

Medium-bodied, sweet.

Golden yellow in color with inviting aromas of golden apple, citrus, and banana. Sweet, fruity, and floral with rose petal, pear, apple, and peach notes. Delicious with butter pecan ice cream.

Pearmund Cellars

6190 Georgetown Road
Broad Run, VA 20137
(540) 347-3475
www.pearmundcellars.com

After 12 years as the owner of Meriweather Winery, owner and winemaker Chris Pearmund established Pearmund Cellars— a 7500 square foot geothermal winery— in 2003. They now produce about 5000 cases per year of chardonnay, viognier, riesling, cabernet franc, and many other varietals.

Pearmund Late Harvest Dessert Style Vidal 2003, Virginia, 375ml, $16

Beautifully balanced acids and sweetness.

Medium-bodied, sweet.

Delicate, mouth-watering aromas of tropical fruits and violets. Creamy, yet crisp on the palate with medium acids to balance the sweet peach, apricot, maple, and honeysuckle notes. Delicious with carrot cake with cream cheese frosting or pecan pie.

Shadow Canyon Cellars

846 Higuera Street, #5
San Luis Obispo, CA 93401
(805) 781-9400
www.shadowcanyon.com

Owner and winemaker Gary Gibson bought his York Mountain property in 1996 and has been making high quality wines ever since. Both his syrah and his pinot blanc are widely acclaimed, and his syrah grapes have been used for Manfred Krankl's famed Sine Qua Non wines.

Shadow Canyon Cellars Dessert Style Pinot Blanc Paeonia Bien Nacido Vineyards, Santa Maria Valley—Santa Barbara, 375ml, $30

Decadent. A dessert in and of itself.

Medium-bodied, sweet.

Aromas of honey, orange blossom, apricot, and oak. Sweet, buttery and rich with jam, wild honey, and spice notes. Delicious with simple, slightly tart desserts like peach or blackberry pie.

Vino Con Brio

7889 East Harney Lane
Lodi, CA 95240
(209) 369-5392
www.vinoconbrio.com

Mike and Renae Matson and their three adult children own and operate both the winery and Amorosa Inn and Gardens. With winemaker Paul Wofford, they concentrate on zinfandel, Rhone, and Italian varietals.

Vino Con Brio Matzin Late Harvest Zinfandel 2004, Lodi, 375ml, $21

Elegant. Light on its feet.

Full-bodied, sweet.

Aromas of stewed cherry, rhubarb, hay, mint, and raisin notes are followed with intense cherry, blackberry, and Dr. Pepper. Very silky and elegant. Enjoy with mission fig tartlets or blackberry cobbler.

Wilson Vineyards

50400 Gaffney Road
Post Office Box 307
Clarksburg, CA 95612
(916) 744-1456
www.wilsonvineyards.com

Now in their third generation, the Wilson family vineyards are under the stewardship of Ken, who sells some of the fruit to big name as well as cult California producers. His sister Sandra is in charge of marketing.

**Wilson Vineyards Late Harvest Chenin Blanc
2002, Clarksburg, 375ml, $20**

Good value. Exotic.

Medium-bodied, off dry.

Peach, cherimoya, star fruit, honeydew, beeswax, caramel, toffee, and
honey notes. Beautifully balanced with a silky texture and clean finish.
Delicious with mango crème brûlée or with seared foie gras.

Work Vineyard

3190 Highway 128
Calistoga, CA 94515
(707) 942-0251
www.workvineyard.com

Karen and Henry Work moved to Napa Valley from San Diego in
1974 and immersed themselves in the wine business. In 1987, they
purchased a three-acre sauvignon blanc vineyard in Calistoga and
became grape growers, selling to Caymus and Cakebread, amongst
others. In 2001, they launched their own label with a 230 case
production and today produce about 1200 cases.

**Work Vineyard Late Work Sauvignon Blanc
Naturally Botrytised Dessert Wine Napa Valley,
375ml, $35.00**

Very rare. 593 half bottles produced.

Medium-bodied, sweet.

Honey, apricot, pineapple, rose petal, nutmeg, and almond butter
notes. Decadence balanced with juicy natural acidity. Enjoy alone or
with peach cobbler or baklava.

Direct Shipment Resources

On page 233 is a table that shows which states are reciprocal (shipping always permitted with other reciprocal states), limited (shipping usually permitted, but with some restrictions), and prohibited.

The list of reciprocal, limited, and prohibited states should be used only as a guideline. It should not be considered legal advice.

For more detailed information, check out the websites below. They contain useful information regarding the process of direct shipment and its legal status in all 50 states.

Be sure to check the sites frequently, as laws are continually changing. Your state may also have information on its own government-sponsored agriculture site.

www.freethegrapes.org—A non-profit organization dedicated to promoting wine trade among the 50 states. Contains up-to-date information on developments in direct shipment laws, as well as ways for you to get involved in your state.

www.pacificresearch.org — Site of the Pacific Research Institute, a think tank which has published informative articles on direct shipment. An excellent source for research purposes.

www.wineinstitute.org — The public policy advocacy association of California wineries. Contains information on direct shipment, the latest news updates, and resources for legal information. They suggest that for up-to-the-minute information, consumers should contact the Wine Institute's State Relations Department at (415) 356-7530.

State Shipping Laws[1]

Current as of May 31, 2006

Reciprocal[2]	Shipping limited	Shipping prohibited
Colorado	Alaska	Alabama
Hawaii	Arizona	Arkansas
Idaho	California	Delaware
Illinois	Connecticut	Florida
Iowa	Georgia	Indiana
Minnesota	Louisiana	Kansas
Missouri	Michigan	Kentucky
New Mexico	Nebraska	Maine
Oregon	Nevada	Maryland
Washington	New Hampshire	Massachusetts
West Virginia	New York	Mississippi
Wisconsin	North Carolina	Montana
	North Dakota	New Jersey
	Ohio	Oklahoma
	Rhode Island	Pennsylvania
	South Carolina	South Dakota
	Texas	Tennessee
	Virginia	Utah
	Washington, D.C.	Vermont
	Wyoming	

---

[1] This information was provided by the Wine Institute. See www.wineinstitute.org for more information.

[2] Reciprocity refers to a legislative agreement by which two states recognize mutual shipping rights. For example, wineries in Hawaii can ship to Washington consumers because Washington wineries can ship to consumers in Hawaii.

INDEX

CREDITS

Authors:

Master Sommelier Catherine Fallis is founder and President of **Planet Grape LLC**, a company committed to bringing the joy of wine, food, and good living into the lives of everyday people. Catherine is creator of the *grape goddess guides to good living*, a series of books, television presentations, seminars, and e-learning programs. The fifth woman in the world to become a Master Sommelier, grape goddess Catherine Fallis is still very much down-to-earth.

Robert M. Cohen, a wine writer and lawyer, has been Editor At Large for *Touring and Tasting Magazine* for the past 10 years, where he has penned numerous lifestyle and wine pieces. Additionally, he has written articles for the *Insider's Wine Guide* and *The Journal of Italian Food* and is past Vice President of the California Restaurant Writers Association.

Since the early 1990s, he has traveled widely in Italy and the U.S.in search of the perfect Italian meal (when not practicing law). He lives in Los Angeles.

Text: Catherine Fallis and Robert M. Cohen

Project Editor: Lisa M. Tooker

Design and symbols: Richard Garnas

Layout and production: Patty Holden

Photography: Bucci, Bernardo/Corbis: 2-3; Harwood, Mark/Getty Images: cover; O'Rear, Charles/Corbis: 13 (bottom), 18-21, 22-23 (top), 24-35, 36-37 (top), 38-39, 40-41 (top), 42-43 (top), 44-45 (top), 46-49, 50-51 (top), 52-53 (top), 54-55 (top), 56-69, 70-71 (top), 224-231; Rondel, Benjamin/Corbis: 72-113, 114-115 (top), 116-127, 128-129 (top), 130-131 (top), 132-143, 144-145 (top), 146-147, 148-149 (top), 150-151 (top), 152-153 (top), 154-155, 156-157 (top), 158-175, 176-177 (top), 178-181, 182-183 (top), 184-197, 198-199 (top), 200-205, 206-207 (top), 208-223; Rowan, Bob/Corbis: 4-5 (top), 6-11, 12-13 (top), 14-17, 36 (bottom), 40 (middle), 42 (middle), 45 (middle), 51 (middle), 52 (middle), 55 (bottom), 70 (middle), 115 (middle), 128 (middle), 131 (bottom), 145 (bottom), 150 (middle), 152 (bottom), 157 (bottom), 177 (middle), 182 (bottom), 199 (bottom), 207 (bottom), 232-248; Sanford, Ron/Corbis: 4-5 (bottom); Watts, Ron/Corbis: title page

ISBN 1-59637-091-2

Printed in China